Along UTA Lines

Ulster's rail network in the 1960s

Ian McLarnon Sinclair

Colourpoint

6 5 4 3 2 1

© Ian McLarnon Sinclair
and Colourpoint Books
Newtownards 2002

Designed by Colourpoint Books, Newtownards
Printed by Nicholson and Bass Ltd

ISBN 1 898392 77 3

Ian McLarnon Sinclair is from Bangor, Co
Down and has been a lifelong railway
enthusiast. As a student of the Ulster
Polytechnic (now University of Ulster) he
worked for five summers on Northern Ireland
Railways in its Signals and Telegraphs
department. He is employed by BBC NI and
has produced a number of radio documentaries
on transport subjects. He is a former member
of North Down Borough Council, where he
took an active interest in transport issues, and
was also closely involved in the recent 'Save
Our Railways' campaign in Northern Ireland.

Photo Credits

All photographs, except where otherwise credited, are © Crown Copyright. Reproduced
by permission of the Controller of Her Majesty's Stationery Office.

Colourpoint Books
Unit D5, Ards Business Centre
Jubilee Road
NEWTOWNARDS
County Down
Northern Ireland
BT23 4YH
Tel: (028) 9182 0505
Fax: (028) 9182 1900
E-mail: Info@colourpoint.co.uk
Web-site: www.colourpoint.co.uk

Cover Photographs

Front cover: Ex GNR(I) UG class 0-6-0 No 49 enters Platform 4, Portadown, with a
Sunday school excursion bound for Bangor, 19 June 1965.   *Norman Johnston*

Rear cover, top: Newtownstewart featured all the hallmarks of a typical GNR(I) station.
On the down platform was a typical WH Mills' building in yellow brick whilst on the up
side were the ubiquitous GNR(I) signal cabin and wooden shelter. The large stone
building behind the up platform was the goods shed.   *John Laird*

Rear cover, bottom: This typical NCC signal cabin controlled the once busy station at
Larne and stood between the railway and Larne Lough. The area behind the cabin has since
been reclaimed and in 1974 the railway was diverted onto it and the old station cleared
away. The new Larne Town is a simple single platform affair with no need for a cabin.

Contents

Abbreviations

BBR	Belfast and Ballymena Railway	INWR	Irish North Western Railway
BCDR	Belfast and County Down Railway	LCR	Londonderry and Coleraine Railway
BLR	Ballymena and Larne Railway	LER	Londonderry and Enniskillen Railway
BNCR	Belfast and Northern Counties Railway		
BBCPJR	Ballymena, Ballymoney, Coleraine and Portrush Junction Railway	LMS	London, Midland and Scottish Railway
BHBR	Belfast, Holywood and Bangor Railway	MR	Midland Railway
		NCC	Northern Counties Committee
CLR	Carrickfergus and Larne Railway	NIR	Northern Ireland Railways
CDRJC	County Donegal Railway Joint Committee	NWRR	Newry, Warrenpoint and Rostrevor Railway
CIÉ	Coras Iompair Éireann	PDR	Portadown and Dungannon Railway
DER	Dundalk and Enniskillen Railway	PDOJR	Portadown, Dungannon and Omagh Junction Railway
DCR	Derry Central Railway	UR	Ulster Railway
GNR(I)	Great Northern Railway (Ireland)	UTA	Ulster Transport Authority

Introduction and Acknowledgements

All too often at a talk about railways the speaker has projected a photograph on the screen. Hidden, tantalisingly, behind the locomotive is a glimpse of a piece of railway infrastructure removed many years ago. In the ensuing discussion the speaker laments that he had not taken the time, or spared the film, to photograph that feature.

In the 1960s, film was expensive and steam was rapidly disappearing from Ulster's shrinking railway network. The photographer's priority was to record as many of the locomotives as he could. Buildings and other aspects of infrastructure usually 'just got in the way'. Fortunately, though, there were a few enthusiasts whose interests did extend beyond the locomotives and who had the foresight to record, on film, our 'built' railway heritage.

Two such people were the late Dr ERR Green and Dr WA McCutcheon. Dr Green was, in the early 1960s, lecturing in the History Department at the University of Manchester. He took a keen interest in the industrial archaeology of his native Northern Ireland and published a book on the subject. He was also a member of the Ancient Monuments Advisory Council, which advised the Ministry of Finance at Stormont, and chaired its Industrial Archaeology sub-committee. In this capacity he persuaded the Ministry of Finance to engage someone, initially for three years, to go around Northern Ireland and record every aspect of it.

Dr McCutcheon, a geography teacher at the Royal Belfast Academical Institution (and later Director of the Ulster Museum) was seconded to the job. Between 1963 and 1968 he researched the subject in great detail and visited every corner of Northern Ireland, taking some 27,000 photographs, including several thousand relating to transport. In 1980 Her Majesty's Stationery Office published his marvellous reference book, *The Industrial Archaeology of Northern Ireland*, which was a result of this work.

In early 2000 I was looking for some pictures to accompany an article about Bangor station, demolished during the previous summer. Mark Kennedy, Railways Curator at the Ulster Folk and Transport Museum, pointed me in the direction of the 'McCutcheon Collection', now in the care of Built Heritage, Environment and Heritage Service (DOE NI) in Hill Street, Belfast. Here was a marvellous selection of photographs, many of which had never previously been published, including numerous views of stations across Northern Ireland.

Of particular interest to me was a selection showing Holywood. I could just remember it from my childhood days in the town before much of the station was destroyed by fire, but I had never managed to find a decent photograph of the buildings. All of a sudden, in front of me, was a detailed study of them, depicting many features which I could just recall or had only heard about.

At that time the collection had not been catalogued (that process is now underway) and was not readily available to the general public. That seemed a great shame, and soon the idea of a book based on the railway photographs in the archive came to mind. At least then a small proportion of them would be in the public domain. Thanks are due to Terence Reeves-Smyth and his colleagues at the Environment and Heritage Service for access to the collection and producing the prints.

In order to present a complete picture of the railway stations of that period – the early 1960s – I have also used material from other sources, in particular Stations UK's vast archive which covers railways from all parts of the British Isles. The other photographers whose work features in this book are Norman Bailey, Drew Donaldson, John Edgington, Des FitzGerald, Brian Griffith, Norman Johnston, John Laird (now the Lord Laird of Artigarvan), Dr EM Patterson, Craig Robb, William Robb MBE, Drew Sucksmith, Richard Whitford, and Derek Young. I am also indebted to Charles Friel for access to his comprehensive collection of Irish railway photographs, particularly those taken by Dr Patterson.

Their assistance has enabled me to feature every railway station which was open during this period, together with many closed stations and halts along the surviving UTA passenger lines.

In the course of this work many others have helped solve puzzles or provided me with additional information – Robert Crangle, James Donaghy, Alec Esdale, Roy Forsythe, Denis Grimshaw, John Harcourt, Kieran Hughes, Billy McCormick, Thomas McGauran, Harry Mulholland, Michael Pollard, John Richardson, John Sinclair, Ian Wilson and Jack Woods. Alec Esdale, Charles Friel, Billy McCormick and Michael Pollard undertook the burden of checking my text. I am also grateful to Joyce and Norman Topley, Mark Kennedy and Laurence Smith for their assistance with station diagrams.

During the year in which this book was being prepared I visited all the sites featured, accompanied by either Roy Forsythe or Henry Sinclair, and met many people who kindly gave us the necessary directions to the sites or various other pieces of information. Thanks are also due to the staff at the Public Record Office of Northern Ireland, Ordnance Survey of Northern Ireland, Belfast Central Library and the South Eastern Education and Library Board's library headquarters for assistance with research.

Finally, I must record my appreciation to Norman Johnston and Colourpoint Books for their support of this project.

The period covered by this book, 1960–65, must, with hindsight, be one of the most interesting in Ulster's railway history. It was a time of consolidation after the widespread closures of the 1950s. Many passenger services were operated by modern diesel railcars, some of which were designed by the UTA itself during that organisation's pioneering days, but others still depended on an ageing fleet of steam locomotives. In most places the infrastructure provided by the former railway companies (much of it dating back to the previous century) survived, largely intact, on those lines which the UTA still operated.

However, time was moving on and by the end of the decade there would be more changes to the network which, in many cases, would alter it beyond all recognition. Another round of closures, in 1965, reduced the railway system to its present size. The monolithic UTA disappeared a few years later, replaced by a new company called Northern Ireland Railways, heralding a new era in rail travel. The 1970s brought modernisation of what remained of our rail network – steam disappeared from the scene, new diesel locomotives and railcars were bought, many miles of track and signalling were renewed, and some lines even reopened.

But some of the biggest changes were in the stations. With the withdrawal of the last goods trains on local services, the sheds were closed and yards ripped up. Modern signalling meant that there was no longer a need for signal cabins as we knew them. The introduction of conductors who sold tickets on the trains led to the reduction of many stations to unmanned halts, the often extensive buildings giving way to simple open shelters. Other stations were replaced by modern ones at new locations, most significantly in Belfast where all three original termini have disappeared. The IRA bombing campaign, which plagued NIR for most of its existence as an independent company, also took its toll on our railway heritage.

This book is not about the trains but about the stations which they served and which were, in so many places, a focal point of the community; reflecting the importance that our railway system once had right across Northern Ireland. Through these photographs we can see the major contribution the old railway companies made to what we now call our 'built heritage', and marvel at the influence of a very few men – most notably Sir Charles and John Lanyon, Berkeley Deane Wise and William Henry Mills – in that architecture.

To those of you who travelled by train along the UTA lines and used these stations, I hope that this book will bring back happy memories; to those of you who were not fortunate to experience the rail network before that final round of closures and subsequent modernisation, I hope that it will arouse a greater interest in an aspect of Ulster's railway heritage which has been so often been ignored.

Ian McLarnon Sinclair
Bangor
February 2002

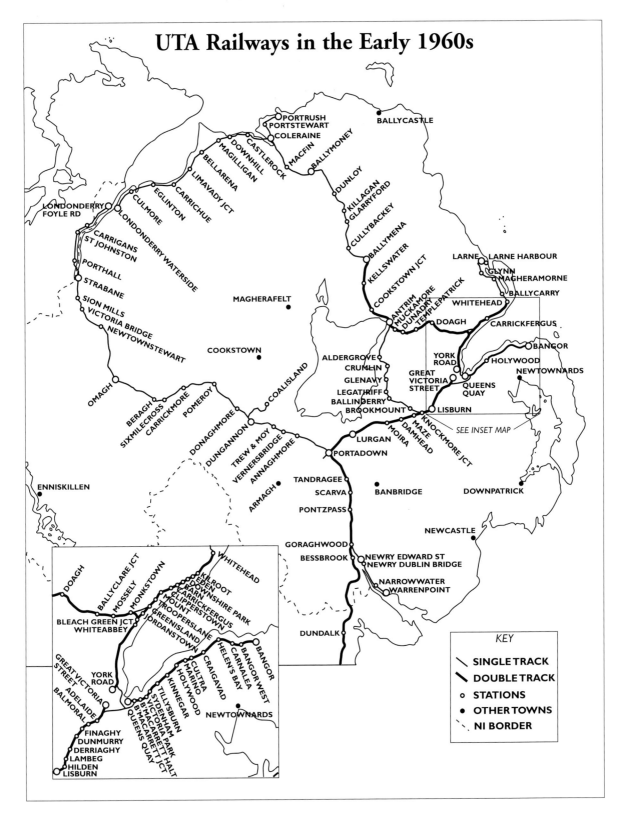

UTA Railways in the Early 1960s

PORTRUSH
PORTSTEWART
COLERAINE
BALLYCASTLE
CASTLEROCK
DOWNHILL
MACFIN
MAGILLIGAN
BALLYMONEY
BELLARENA
DUNLOY
LIMAVADY JCT
KILLAGAN
GLARRYFORD
CARRICHUE
EGLINTON
CULLYBACKEY
CULMORE
BALLYMENA
LONDONDERRY FOYLE RD
LONDONDERRY WATERSIDE
KELLSWATER
CARRIGANS ST JOHNSTON
COOKSTOWN JCT
LARNE LARNE HARBOUR
GLYNN
MAGHERAMORNE
PORTHALL
MAGHERAFELT
ANTRIM
MUCKAMORE
DUNADRY
TEMPLEPATRICK
BALLYCARRY
STRABANE
WHITEHEAD
SION MILLS
DOAGH
VICTORIA BRIDGE
CARRICKFERGUS
NEWTOWNSTEWART
COOKSTOWN
YORK ROAD
BANGOR
ALDERGROVE
HOLYWOOD
CRUMLIN
NEWTOWNARDS
OMAGH
GLENAVY
GREAT VICTORIA STREET
BERAGH
COALISLAND
LEGATIRIFF
QUEENS QUAY
SIXMILECROSS
POMEROY
BALLINDERRY
CARRICKMORE
BROOKMOUNT
LISBURN
DONAGHMORE
KNOCKMORE JCT
DUNGANNON
TREW & MOY
MAZE
DAMHEAD
VERNERSBRIDGE
LURGAN
MOIRA
SEE INSET MAP
ANNAGHMORE
ENNISKILLEN
PORTADOWN
TANDRAGEE
ARMAGH
SCARVA
BANBRIDGE
DOWNPATRICK
PONTZPASS
NEWCASTLE
GORAGHWOOD
BESSBROOK
NEWRY EDWARD ST
NEWRY DUBLIN BRIDGE
NARROWWATER
WARRENPOINT
DUNDALK

Inset Map

WHITEHEAD
DOAGH
BALLYCLARE JCT
KILROOT
MOSSELY
EDEN
MONKSTOWN
DOWNSHIRE PARK
BARN
CARRICKFERGUS
CLIPPERSTOWN
TROOPERSTOWN
MOUNT
GREENISLAND
JORDANSTOWN
BLEACH GREEN JCT
WHITEABBEY
BANGOR
CULTRA
CRAIGAVAD
HELEN'S BAY
CARNALEA
BANGOR WEST
GREAT VICTORIA STREET
MARINO
HOLYWOOD
KINNEGAR
YORK ROAD
TILLYSBURN
SYDENHAM
NEWTOWNARDS
ADELAIDE
VICTORIA PARK
B'MACARRETT HALT
BALMORAL
B'MACARRETT
QUEENS QUAY
FINAGHY
DUNMURRY
DERRIAGHY
LAMBEG
HILDEN
LISBURN

KEY

\ SINGLE TRACK

\ DOUBLE TRACK

○ STATIONS

● OTHER TOWNS

⌐⌐ NI BORDER

1 The Great Northern Main Line

We begin our tour of the Ulster Transport Authority's passenger lines of the 1960s at Belfast Great Victoria Street station. Originally named Glengall Place, this was Belfast's first terminus, opened in 1839 by the Ulster Railway, together with its line to Lisburn. It was replaced in 1848, an important year for railways in Belfast, by the building illustrated here. Amalgamation with other railway companies in 1876 led to the Ulster Railway becoming part of the Great Northern Railway (Ireland). The GNR(I) made many improvements to the station, including construction of the porte cochère which proudly bore the company's name. A newspaper vendor has set up his stall to the right of the main entrance. In October 1968 the portion of the building illustrated was demolished to make way for the Europa Hotel. An uninspiring wooden entrance façade was squeezed in between the surviving wing, which housed the Grosvenor Rooms restaurant, and the hotel. The station was replaced by Belfast Central in April 1976 and demolished soon after.

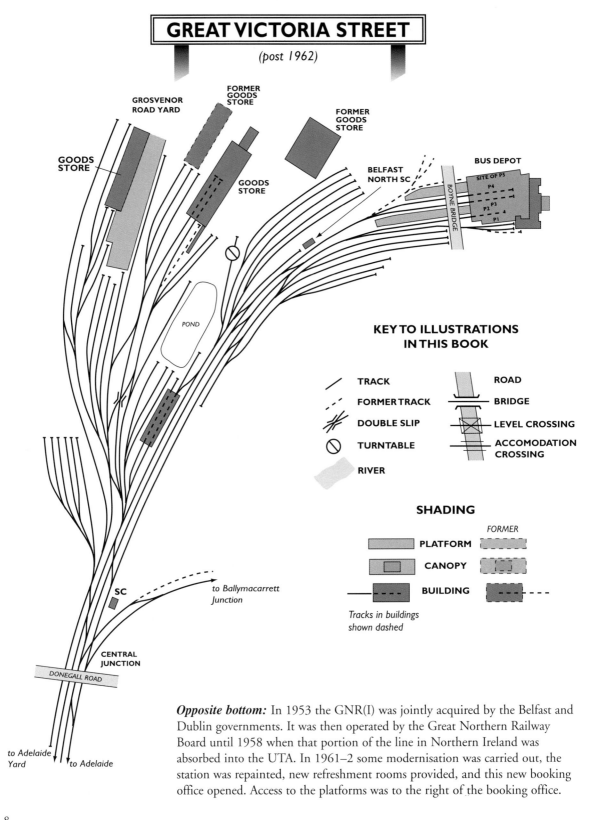

GREAT VICTORIA STREET

(post 1962)

GROSVENOR
ROAD YARD

FORMER
GOODS
STORE

FORMER
GOODS
STORE

BUS DEPOT

SITE OF P5

GOODS
STORE

GOODS
STORE

BELFAST
NORTH SC

BOYNE BRIDGE

P4
P3
P2
P1
4

POND

KEY TO ILLUSTRATIONS
IN THIS BOOK

TRACK

ROAD

FORMER TRACK

BRIDGE

DOUBLE SLIP

LEVEL CROSSING

TURNTABLE

ACCOMODATION
CROSSING

RIVER

SHADING

FORMER

PLATFORM

CANOPY

BUILDING

*Tracks in buildings
shown dashed*

SC

to Ballymacarrett
Junction

CENTRAL
JUNCTION

DONEGALL ROAD

to Adelaide
Yard

to Adelaide

Opposite bottom: In 1953 the GNR(I) was jointly acquired by the Belfast and Dublin governments. It was then operated by the Great Northern Railway Board until 1958 when that portion of the line in Northern Ireland was absorbed into the UTA. In 1961–2 some modernisation was carried out, the station was repainted, new refreshment rooms provided, and this new booking office opened. Access to the platforms was to the right of the booking office.

As the railway network grew, the number of platforms increased from two to five. The original UR platforms, later numbered 3 and 4, became island platforms. In GNR(I) days an overall roof was built over Platforms 2 to 5. The short Platform 1 was a later addition and was outside the main building. It was popularly known as the 'motor' platform as it was often used by steam railmotors on short workings to Lisburn. The brackets on the pillars supporting the roof featured a monogram of the company's initials, an arrangement replicated at other stations including Platform 1 at Lisburn, where they can still be seen, and at Lurgan and Londonderry Foyle Road.

The wrought-iron platform barrier was replaced by one in similar style to the booking office. Enterprise passengers usually used the left-hand gate. The UTA's coat of arms can be seen above it. At this time trains were still running to Newry, Warrenpoint, and along the 'Derry Road'.

Platform 5 was the Enterprise platform in GNR(I) days but in 1962, as part of the UTA's alterations, it was filled in to create the bus station. Great Victoria Street station was therefore the city's first joint road and rail terminus, an arrangement broken between 1976 and 1995. Platforms 2 and 3 were extended and Enterprise trains transferred to Platform 2 where a new customs hall was built. Platform 1, at the far side of the complex, was also extended. Distinctive ex-BCDR concrete coping stones with a 'criss-cross' pattern were used on this extension. Occupying the site of the former Platform 5 are, nearest the camera, a Post Office van, a PS1 bus and, in the distance, some taxi cabs.

A feature of Great Victoria Street station was the 'Boyne Bridge' which carried, and indeed still carries, Durham Street over the platforms. In the early days there was just a level crossing here, and this is the second bridge, completed in 1936. Trains returned here in 1995 after an absence of almost 20 years, the right-hand span crossing the new, smaller, terminus, while buses now run under the central and left-hand spans.

As this photograph shows, steam and diesel operated side by side in the early 1960s, indeed steam in Northern Ireland outlasted steam on CIÉ or British Rail. The locomotive at the head of the train in Platform 3 is No 91, ex-LMS(NCC) 2-6-0 'Mogul' *The Bush*, which is shunting a wagon off the back of a railcar. The photographer is standing below Belfast North signal cabin, which controlled all movements in and out of Great Victoria Street. The building to the far right is Murray's tobacco factory, still a familiar sight to railway passengers. On the left are some good examples of GNR(I) semaphore signals. Behind the railing is the new bus depot.

ADELAIDE

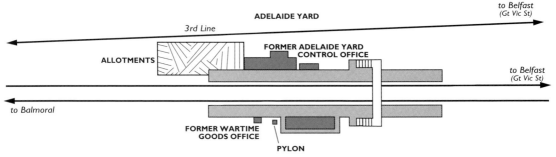

ADELAIDE YARD

to Belfast
(Gt Vic St)

3rd Line

ALLOTMENTS

FORMER ADELAIDE YARD
CONTROL OFFICE

to Belfast
(Gt Vic St)

to Balmoral

FORMER WARTIME
GOODS OFFICE

PYLON

Soon after departing from Belfast, trains passed Central Junction where the Belfast Central Railway trailed in on the up (Lisburn-bound) side. It opened in 1876 but only enjoyed a short-lived passenger service. Its principal use was for goods transfers between the city's three railways and passenger excursions from the GNR(I) system to Bangor. The first halt we reach is Adelaide, close to Windsor Park football stadium. Indeed, it was known as Adelaide and Windsor when it opened in 1897. Adelaide was then a neat suburban station with this wooden building on the up side. Above the door is a cast-iron station nameplate. The GNR(I) placed these at intervals along its platforms, frequently on lamp-posts, giving passengers who missed the large nameboard additional notice of which station they had arrived at. Beyond the building is a pylon which carried internal telephone lines from the nearby yard to a small wartime goods control office behind the platform.

Above: Adelaide yard, adjacent to the halt, was built on 60 acres of Belfast's Bog Meadows and included a nine-road shed capable of holding 55 locomotives. There were also coaling, watering and maintenance facilities although the GNR(I)'s main works were at Dundalk, mid-way between Belfast and Dublin. An unusual feature was the triangle of track used to turn locomotives in lieu of a turntable.

This view shows part of the main locomotive shed, very much a GNR(I) building of yellow brick with black, brown and purple brick courses. This is the side nearest the main line, looking from the Lisburn end, with the third line in the foreground. The locomotive shear legs are just visible at the far end of the shed.

Above right: Glimpsing inside the largely empty shed we see No 58 (ex-GNR(I) VS class No 208) *Lagan*. The shed closed on 31 October 1966, and part of the Adelaide site is now occupied by Northern Ireland Railways' freight depot, opened in 1972, and the adjacent Guinness depot. In the 1960s the dwindling goods traffic was still handled at the Grosvenor Road yard, situated closer to the city centre.

One of the GNR(I)'s standard wooden shelters, of which we will see many in the coming pages, served the down platform at Adelaide. The brick building beyond it was originally the control office for the yard, but later used by the stores department. At the far end of the up platform is one of the searchlight signals which replaced most of the semaphore signals between Belfast and Lisburn in 1964. Here, a CIÉ 'B121' class loco heads north on the Enterprise. A 'third line' between the halt and the yard gave access to and from Great Victoria Street station and Grosvenor Road goods yard without congesting the main lines. Adelaide yard was, by now, being used to store and scrap redundant wagons and carriages such as the ex-BCDR bogie coach to the extreme right. The halt was rebuilt in 1973 and, like most suburban halts along the line, now consists of concrete platforms and basic shelters.

DJA Young

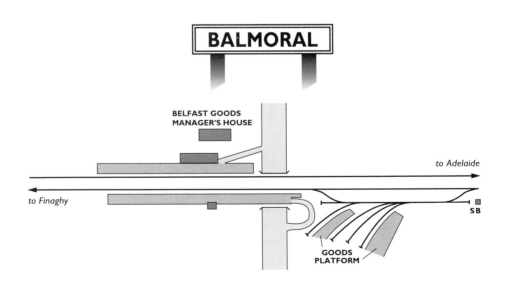

A mile further on we reach Balmoral, situated close to the Royal Ulster Agricultural Society's showgrounds. They were served at one time by sidings off the main line on the up side. The bridge over Stockman's Lane, adjacent to the station, was rebuilt in 1963 and the track level raised. The platforms were also raised, initially by these structures made from old sleepers which were soon replaced by concrete slabs on brick piers. The original stone faces can still be seen.

This substantial building was on the down (Belfast-bound) side. It has now gone but the Belfast Goods Manager's house, behind this platform, still stands as a private dwelling. On the up side the GNR(I) provided a small brick shelter with an arched opening.

CP Friel collection

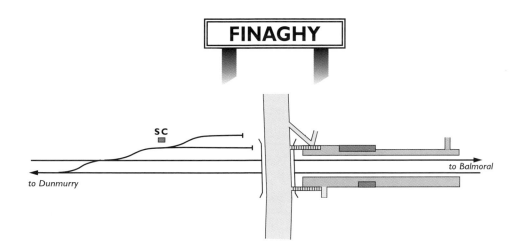

Finaghy was the first of a series of 'railmotor' halts opened in 1907, served by local push-pull trains running to and from Lisburn. Wooden platforms with the standard design of shelters on each were provided. A simple ticket booth stands beside the shelter on the down side. The photographer is standing on the road bridge, looking towards Belfast. A small goods yard was established behind this bridge, on the down side. As part of the station refurbishment programme of the early 1970s Finaghy was entirely rebuilt with concrete platforms and new shelters.

Stations UK 5835

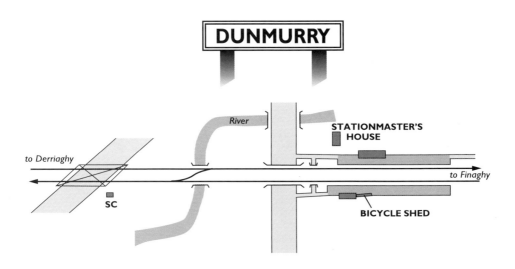

Dunmurry opened in 1839 as the only intermediate station on the line to Lisburn. It was also the last intermediate station on this section of line to be manned. The building we see here was situated on the down platform and has now been replaced by a simple shelter. As the signs on the doors show, Dunmurry still offered separate Ladies' and Gentlemen's waiting rooms. The waiting rooms on the up side became a clothes factory in 1971 but are now used by an office supply company.

A short distance beyond Dunmurry station was this signal cabin, typical of many located around the GNR(I) system. 'Searchlight' signals were introduced between Belfast and Lisburn in 1964, except at Dunmurry where the cabin remained open to control some of this signalling and to operate the crossing gates. The other intermediate cabins were closed. Dunmurry cabin was destroyed by a bomb in 1973, its replacement also being blown up in 1979. The signalling in this area is now controlled by Belfast Central.

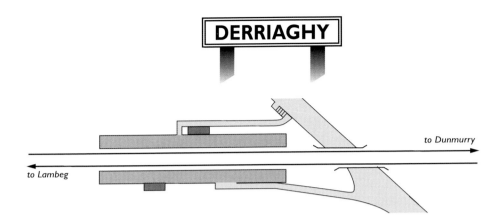

DERRIAGHY

to Dunmurry

to Lambeg

The next 1907 'railmotor' halt was at Derriaghy, closed between 1953 and 1956. Again, wooden platforms were provided. Looking towards Belfast, we see that the down platform had the usual wooden shelter while, during the Second World War, the up side was given a brick shelter. NIR replaced the down platform shelter with a brick one in the early 1970s, but Derriaghy was the last of the halts to be rebuilt, lasting largely as shown here into the 1980s.

Stations UK 5833

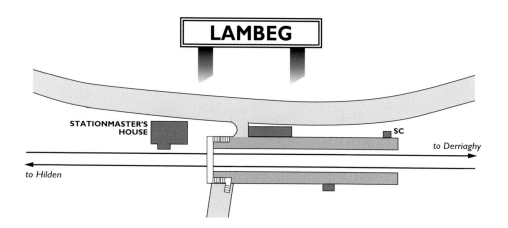

Lambeg dates from 1877. It was a well kept station, with its main building on the down platform and a simple brick shelter on the up, this view being taken from the footbridge which spanned the tracks, looking towards Belfast. Tourism was an important source of income in the early 1960s; the poster in the centre is advertising the UTA's range of 'leading' hotels, most of which have long since disappeared, whilst that on the left is for the former British Railways' ferry from Belfast to Heysham.

The buildings have all been cleared away and metal shelters and a modern footbridge now suffice.

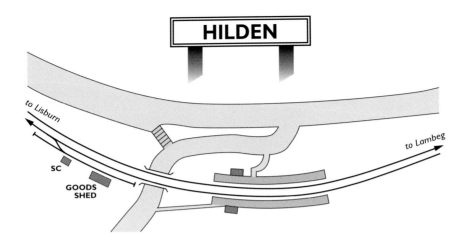

HILDEN

to Lisburn

to Lambeg

SC

GOODS
SHED

Hilden was the last of the 1907 halts, featuring the usual platforms and shelters, seen here looking towards Lisburn. Again, all were replaced in the 1970s refurbishment programme.

Just beyond the halt, on the up side, was a goods siding and store. This served the nearby William Barbour and Son's linen mill, but was used for munitions during the Second World War.

Stations UK 5832

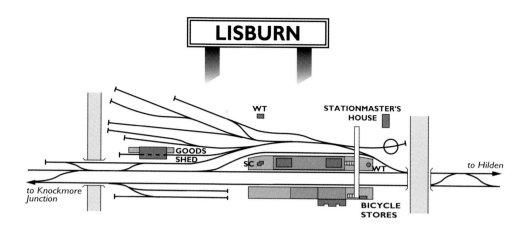

This view of Lisburn station has not changed much over the years. Replacing the original Ulster Railway building in 1878, it features the yellow brick with black, brown and purple ornamental lining favoured by William Henry Mills, the GNR(I)'s chief civil engineer of the time, and used, as we will see, at many other stations on the network. In 1995 Lisburn was extensively restored by NIR and promptly won an architectural heritage award. When the new station was built at Great Victoria Street in the mid-1990s it reflected its GNR(I) heritage by being built in brick of similar colours.

Opposite top: The main building is situated on Platform 1, the up (Dublin-bound) platform. Note the train destination describer – one would be useful at Lisburn today! – and the UTA bus parcels service delivery bicycles, another feature missing from our streets nowadays. The GNR(I) monograms can be clearly seen in the roof brackets. Eason's bookstall and the ticket collector's booth are no longer there, and the sliding door from the main building onto the platform has been replaced, but the scales are still in the same place today.

Opposite bottom: Although the UTA was replacing steam with diesel railcars, CIÉ was moving towards diesel locomotives for their passenger and goods services. B129 is approaching Lisburn from Belfast with the southbound 'Enterprise'. Introduced in 1961, B129 was one of the original batch of American-built General Motors locomotives to enter service in Ireland. So successful were they that GM locomotives now dominate the Irish railway scene; indeed many of the original locomotives remain in service. The covered footbridge has since been replaced by an open structure.

Beyond the footbridge, on Platform 1, are a range of cycle stores which passengers could once rent but which are now long gone. The balloon water-tank at the end of Platform 2 is still used by Railway Preservation Society of Ireland steam locomotives.

Right: As well as being an important station on the Belfast–Dublin line, Lisburn was once kept busy with passengers changing for the Banbridge/Newcastle and Antrim lines. That traffic had gone by the 1960s but Lisburn was also, and indeed still is, the terminus for many local trains from Belfast. To prevent congestion on the main line it was provided with a third platform in the form of a loop off the down line. This view is looking towards Belfast with Platform 2, the down main line, to the right and Platform 3 to the left. The columns supporting the roof are of a much plainer design than those on Platform 1, and lack the GNR(I) monogram. A drinking water fountain is

just visible at the left-hand end of the waiting room wall. Unlike the section of footbridge linking the platforms, that connecting the station with the North Circular Road was not given a roof.

We finish our stop at Lisburn with a look at the unusually shaped, but still typically GNR(I), signal cabin situated at the Dublin end of the island platform. The offset in the front is repeated on the other side. Although it has been disused for some years now, following the installation of colour light signals, the cabin is extant and well maintained.

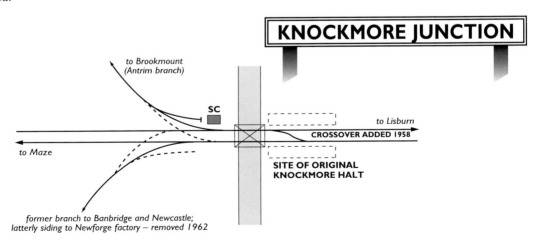

KNOCKMORE JUNCTION

to Brookmount
(Antrim branch)

SC

to Lisburn

CROSSOVER ADDED 1958

to Maze

SITE OF ORIGINAL
KNOCKMORE HALT

former branch to Banbridge and Newcastle;
latterly siding to Newforge factory – removed 1962

A mile west of Lisburn is Knockmore Junction. Prior to its closure in 1956, the Banbridge line diverged to the left, a stump of this line remaining in use until 1961 to serve Newforge factory; it was lifted in 1962. The Antrim line, which we will visit later, swung off to the right. In 1958 the junction was simplified and a facing crossover installed.

A halt was provided at Knockmore Junction for very brief periods in the 1930s and 1940s, the platforms being on the Lisburn side of the level crossing. This was on a different site to the present Knockmore halt which opened in 1974 and is half a mile nearer Lisburn, at the Ballinderry Road bridge.

Left: The distinctive cabin at Knockmore Junction was built in 1887 and is in the style of one of Mills' station buildings rather than the later GNR(I) cabin design. It was built of red brick with yellow and Staffordshire blue courses. The platform jutting out from the steps enabled the signalman to exchange single line staffs with the branch train's driver or, in the case of railcars, the guard. The wheel used to open and close the level crossing gates is just visible through the right-hand window.

The cabin was demolished in 1977 to enable the junction between the main line and the Antrim branch to be moved to Lisburn. This was facilitated by the construction of a third line which passes over the site of the cabin.

Looking inside, we see the lever frame used to control points and signals. Beyond is the wheel which operated the crossing gates. The instruments on the shelf above the levers include signal repeaters and three track-circuit occupancy indicators.

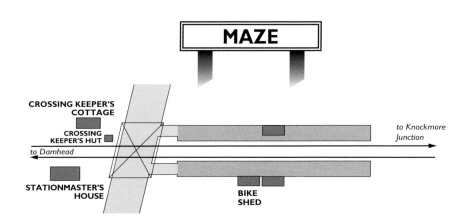

Opposite top: The station at Maze opened in 1895, an unusual feature being the use of wood along some of the top edge of the brick-faced platforms, instead of granite or concrete coping stones. On the down platform is another of those distinctive wooden shelters, whilst a small brick building and corrugated iron bicycle shed served the up side. In this photograph we have a good view of the oil lamps mounted on wooden posts. Behind the photographer, at the Portadown end of the halt, is the level crossing. Beyond it, the stationmaster's house was alongside the up line and a crossing keeper's cottage was provided on the down side; both are still lived in. Maze closed in 1974 but the platforms and remains of the buildings are still there.   *Stations UK 5716*

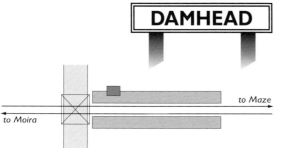

Midway between Maze and Damhead was Broomhedge halt. Both it and Damhead opened in 1935, but Broomhedge only lasted until 1953 and few traces of it remain. The platforms at both stations were faced with wooden sleepers. At Damhead this pre-cast concrete shelter was provided on the down platform, an unusual feature for a GNR(I) station, although the company did use this material in its latter days. Some passengers have left their bicycles sitting on the up platform – there was no shed for them here; this wouldn't be done nowadays! Damhead closed in 1973 although the ruins of the platforms and shelter can still be seen.

Stations UK 6230

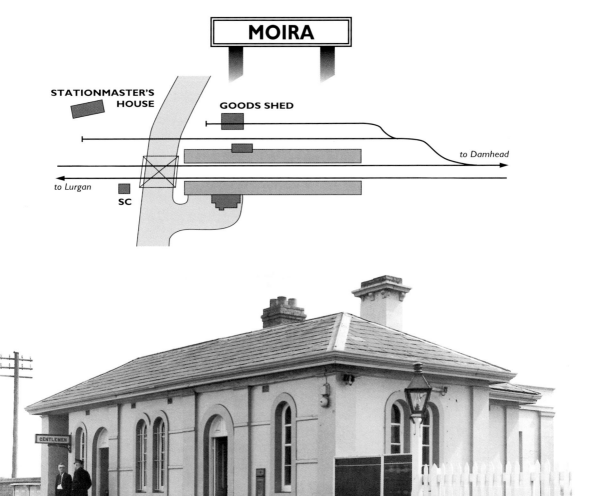

MOIRA

STATIONMASTER'S
HOUSE

GOODS SHED

to Damhead

to Lurgan

SC

The main building on the up platform at Moira is the oldest station building surviving in Northern Ireland. It was built by the Ulster Railway for the opening of its extension to Lurgan in 1841. At platform level it provided a booking office (its windows are protected by bars), ladies' and gents' waiting rooms and parcels storage. It is now in the care of the Environment and Heritage Service of the Department of the Environment which restored it in 1991.

As the track at Moira is on an embankment the building has a deep basement which, when the station opened, provided living accommodation for the stationmaster. The GNR(I) signal cabin, which can be seen on the far side of the level crossing, closed in 1984. It was moved to a new location to the right of the photographer during restoration of the station. This area has been raised in level and is now a car park, Moira having become an important 'Park and Ride' station in recent years.

The GNR(I) later replaced the basic basement living-quarters by this rather more salubrious station house. It is a good example of the many built by the company. An old goods-wagon body has made its way into the garden as a shed. With the closure of many lines in the 1950s and 1960s, and the withdrawal of old rolling stock, carriage and wagon bodies could be seen in use all over the countryside for a variety of domestic and agricultural purposes, and indeed many still survive. The former goods yard, including the house, is now used as a depot by the DOE Environment and Heritage Service.

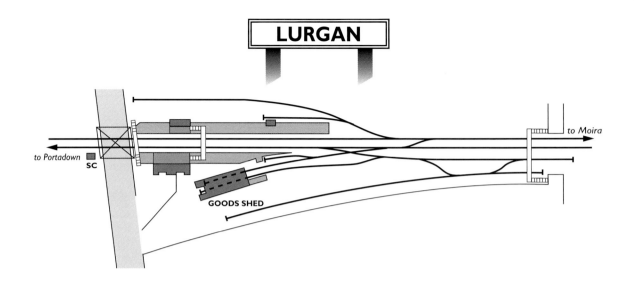

LURGAN

to Portadown

SC

GOODS SHED

to Moira

The main building at Lurgan, again on the up platform, was in much the same style as that at Lisburn, albeit on a smaller scale and built almost twenty years later. The goods depot was situated to the right and, as at many stations, the UTA used part of the forecourt and goods yard for its buses. This building, those on the down platform and the signal cabin were destroyed in various bomb attacks throughout the 1970s. A modern structure, twice rebuilt after bombs, now occupies this site. In 1970 Lurgan was also named Craigavon East, but this name was later dropped.

At the Portadown end of the station is a level crossing, and beyond that the signal cabin once stood. The crossing was unusual in that although it had four conventional gates, operated by a wheel in the cabin, it was also protected by a set of ordinary traffic lights and an electric bell. In 1981 a hydraulic system was installed to operate the gates. This proved unsuccessful and the gates were eventually replaced by full lifting barriers. The footbridge enabled pedestrians to cross the tracks when the level crossing was closed against the road.

The down platform was accessed by a covered footbridge; the bridge numberplate '256' can be clearly seen. The bridges were numbered from Dublin Amiens Street (now Connolly Station), formerly the GNR(I)'s headquarters. Waiting facilities were provided in this attractive wooden building, but in order to accommodate Belfast-bound commuters in rush hour another wooden shelter was provided further along the platform.

PORTADOWN

NORTH

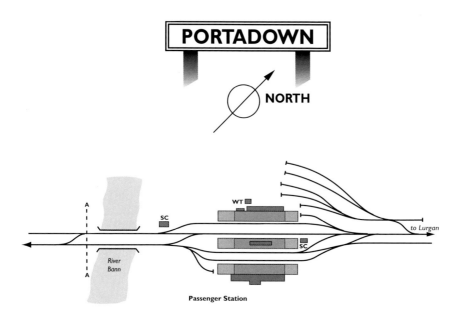

WT

SC

A

River
Bann

A

to Lurgan

SC

Passenger Station

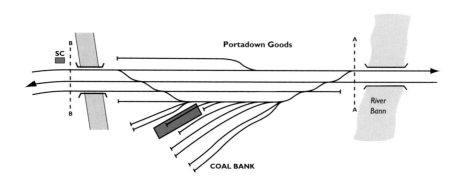

B

SC

Portadown Goods

A

River
Bann

B

A

COAL BANK

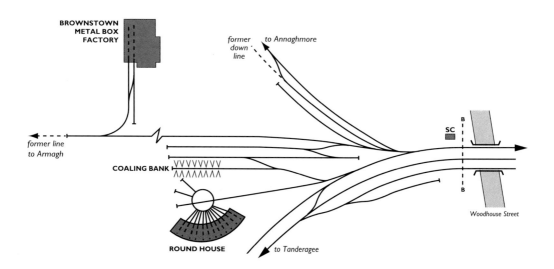

BROWNSTOWN
METAL BOX
FACTORY

former
down
line

to Annaghmore

SC

B

former line
to Armagh

COALING BANK

B

Woodhouse Street

ROUND HOUSE

to Tanderagee

This grand entrance porch led to Portadown's third station. The original opened in 1842 at Watson Street, to the east of the River Bann. With the extension of the line to Armagh in 1848, a new station was built at Woodhouse Street to the west of the river and where the present station stands. As Portadown developed as an important stopping place and junction, a larger passenger facility was needed. Woodhouse Street did not offer scope for expansion so, although it was more convenient to the town centre, it was replaced in 1863 by this building, close to the site of the original and designed by Sir John Macneill. Macneill's station was replaced by the present one in 1970; it was also known at that time as Craigavon West.

Entering the building we find ourselves in the booking hall, little changed over 100 years. Perhaps the only difference, apart from the UTA posters, is that one is invited to book a flight on British European Airways!

Portadown was a busy junction, earning itself the title 'Hub of the North'. After crossing the Bann, the line divided in three, the original Ulster Railway continuing straight on to Armagh and Clones, the main line diverging to the left and heading south to Dublin, and the 'Derry Road', veering right and northwards towards the Maiden City.

When first built, there were just two platforms, later numbered 1 and 4, which were linked by a subway. In 1900 the island platform, numbers 2 and 3, opened along with a new subway which served all platforms. The earlier one, which only served Platforms 1 and 4, was closed in 1960. In 1920 the overall roof was replaced by canopies.

Ex-GNR(I) locomotive No 171 *Slieve Gullion* is at the head of a short train in Platform 2. Although still bearing CIÉ initials, No 171 had, by this time, transferred to the UTA.

This view is of Platform 1, looking west towards the river, on which were the stationmaster's office, parcels office and cloakrooms. At the Belfast end, the Post Office had facilities in a two-storey building which was part of the 1842 station. A buffet and bookstall were provided on the island platform, together with a waiting room which can be seen to the right of the locomotive.

Above: Crossing to the far platform (No 4), we find CIÉ locomotive B158 arriving with a southbound 'Lough Derg' special from the 'Derry Road'. These trains carried pilgrims to and from Omagh; from there they were brought by bus to visit a shrine on an island on Lough Derg, near Pettigo in Co Donegal. With the closure of Goraghwood in January 1965, the UK Customs post was moved to Platform 4 in Portadown. No 171 and its train are still at Platform 2, providing a connection from the 'pilgrim' train to Belfast.

Here we see the Dublin ends of the platforms. An AEC-built railcar is in Platform 1, while B158 has run round its train and is ready to continue its journey south. B158 was one of the second batch of General Motors locomotives to arrive in Ireland. Unlike the earlier class, which had cabs at one end only, these, and all future GMs, were fitted with cabs at both ends. The sentry box on the island platform housed a railway telephone which allowed platform staff to quickly talk to the signal cabins or booking office.

Locomotive roundhouses were scarce in Ireland, the only ones on the GNR(I) system being at Portadown and, across the border, at Clones. The Portadown shed was built of reinforced concrete in 1925 and, after closure in 1965, had to be blown up by the army. The advantage of a roundhouse over a conventional locomotive shed was that each engine had its own road and so could be moved in and out at will without being blocked by another. In the shed are, from left to right, an unidentified SG3 class locomotive, No 36 (formerly GNR(I) SG3 class 0-6-0 No 49) and No 49 (ex-GNR(I) UG class 0-6-0 No 149). The doors on the left-hand roads were fitted about 1962 to give some small degree of shelter to fitters and men washing out boilers.

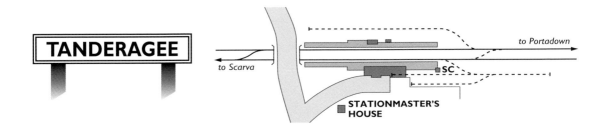

TANDERAGEE

to Portadown

to Scarva

SC

STATIONMASTER'S HOUSE

Located midway between the villages of Tandragee and Gilford, Tanderagee (the GNR(I) generally gave it an extra 'e') was located on the Dublin and Belfast Junction Railway. It completed the link between Drogheda and Portadown in 1852, and the station opened then. At that time it was called Madden Bridge, then Tanderagee and Gilford, and plain Tanderagee from 1894. The station boasted a substantial building on the up platform, which dated back to the opening, a goods shed and traditional GNR(I) signal cabin beyond. A stationmaster's house, now in private ownership, was added behind this platform.

On the down platform is a fine example of a typical wooden shelter of the type used throughout the GNR(I) system. Another cast nameplate can be seen on the end of the building, below the lamp. The station closed in 1965 but is still remembered with affection because its name was given as Tanderagee on one platform and Tandragee on the other! With the exception of the stationmaster's house, all the buildings have since been demolished.

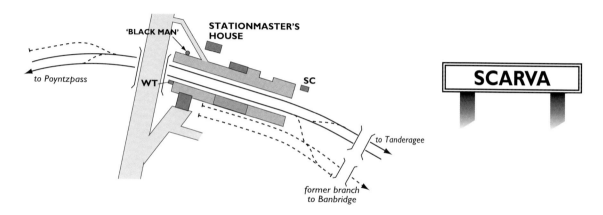

Scarva also opened in 1852, but although it closed to regular trains in 1965 it continued to be used every year on 13 July to facilitate specials, usually in the form of a shuttle service from Portadown, bringing crowds to watch the 'Sham Fight'. This is a re-enactment of the Battle of the Boyne, and on this day the figure of a man cut out of the hedge on the down platform sported a Royal Black Preceptory sash.

The main station building, dating from 1852, was on the up platform, and the GNR(I) later added the stationmaster's house behind the down. Scarva regained a daily service in 1984 but most of these buildings have gone. All that remains today is the stationmaster's house, another private dwelling, and a boarded-up shelter on the down side. There were plans in the 1990s to replace the stone road bridge on which the photographer is standing, but it had an eleventh hour reprieve.

This photograph was taken on 18 July 1964 and shows ex-NCC 2-6-4T locomotive No 50 hauling a passenger train bound for Warrenpoint. By this time the signal cabin near the far end of the down platform (to our left here) had been demolished; it closed in 1962.

Craig Robb

Scarva became a junction in 1859, this time with a branch line to Banbridge (via Laurencetown) which closed in 1955. This view is taken from the down mainline platform and shows the simple island-platform building which served the up main line and, to the far side, the branch. The building on the extreme right was the interchange goods store for traffic to and from the Newry Canal.

POYNTZPASS

Another 1852 station, Poyntzpass had its main building on the down platform. Beyond it the GNR(I) added another of those ubiquitous wooden shelters. On the up side was a stone shelter, still standing but closed off, whilst the down platform buildings have been demolished. Behind the down platform was the goods yard, now used by NIR for loading ballast trains. Although the passenger station was closed between 1965 and 1984, Poyntzpass cabin, just seen to the left of the photograph, remained open. For much of the 1970s, it was the only block post between Portadown and the border, and the cabin also looked after the level crossing on which the photographer is standing. Signalling in the area is now controlled from Portadown, but the GNR(I)-built cabin has been preserved in its original spot.

Stations UK 28203

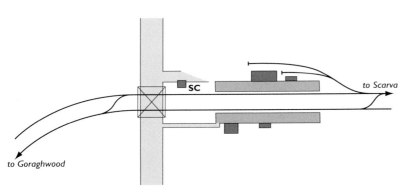

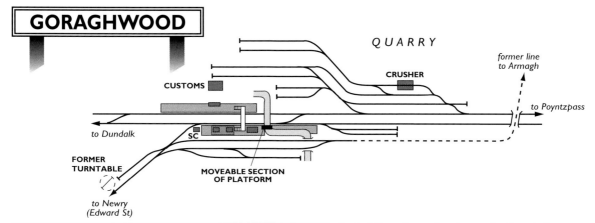

QUARRY

former line
to Armagh

CRUSHER

CUSTOMS

to Poyntzpass

to Dundalk

SC

FORMER
TURNTABLE

MOVEABLE SECTION
OF PLATFORM

to Newry
(Edward St)

GORAGHWOOD
CHANGE FOR
DUNDALK DUBLIN AND BELFAST

Left: "Goraghwood – change for Dundalk, Dublin and Belfast" proclaims this sign, indicating that this was another junction station. It was here that the Newry and Armagh Railway met and crossed the main line by an over bridge at the northern end of the station. This sign was on the branch side of the island platform, the far side of which served the up main line.

Right: This neat wooden building on the island platform provided booking facilities. Goraghwood's importance grew dramatically after the partition of Ireland in 1921 when it became the Northern Ireland customs post. Prior to the introduction of the Enterprise in 1947, all cross-border trains were checked here, sometimes resulting in lengthy delays to services. However, Goraghwood's importance came to an end in 1965 with its closure and the withdrawal of all local services south of Portadown.

Staying on the island platform, this is the canopy which provided cover for those changing to and from the branch train. It was served by Platform 1 which was shorter than Platform 2, the side for up main line trains. There was a level crossing in the middle of Platform 2, bridged by a moveable section of platform when not in use. The crossing gave vehicular access to the GNR(I)'s quarry which provided ballast for the network. Railcar 104 (formerly GNR(I) railcar F) is about to leave for Newry, whilst a steam-hauled CIÉ train is ready to depart for Dublin. The sign we saw previously is situated in the centre of the photograph. The overgrown ruins of Goraghwood are still to be seen, but the granite coping stones along the platforms were recovered and reused at Cultra (on the Bangor line) when it was being refurbished prior to reopening in 1978.

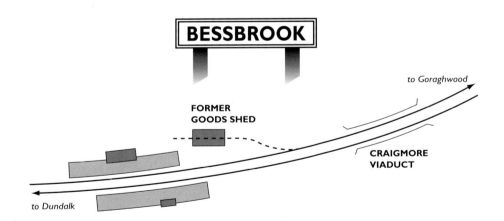

BESSBROOK

to Goraghwood

FORMER
GOODS SHED

CRAIGMORE
VIADUCT

to Dundalk

A couple of miles beyond Goraghwood trains cross the impressive 18-arch Craigmore viaduct. Looking down from the train, passengers can see a footpath which goes under one of the arches; it was, between 1885 and 1948, the trackbed of the electric tramway which linked Newry with the model village of Bessbrook.

Just beyond the viaduct was Bessbrook station. It opened as Newry in 1855 but was later renamed Bessbrook. It closed in 1942 and ceased to be a block post in 1958, but reopened in 1984, once again called Newry! By 1984 the neat station building on the down platform, seen here looking towards Dublin, had gone; on the up platform was the usual wooden shelter. Prior to reopening the platforms were raised and extended; most trains calling at Newry nowadays are Enterprise services. New canopies have been erected, whilst portacabins serve as the booking and waiting facilities; they have been replaced on several occasions after terrorist bombs. A new footbridge has also been built at the Dublin end of the station. The former goods shed, to the right of the photographer, still stands in private commercial use.

Stations UK 28136

Our final view of the GNR(I) main line is of a 'Jeep' hauling a permanent-way train at Meigh, not a station but, from May 1965 until the early 1970s, the last signalling block post in Northern Ireland before trains crossed the border and entered Éire. There the tracks were owned by CIÉ. The signals at Meigh originally protected a set of level-crossing gates, but in 1965 they were upgraded by the UTA to create a new block post which replaced Adavoyle half a mile further south. Adavoyle station had itself closed in 1933. Meigh was reinstated as a temporary block post for a few years from August 1978. Colour light signals and a crossover were installed to permit single-line working when track relaying was in progress in the area. The level crossing is now protected by an automatic half-barrier.

Norman Johnston

2 Newry and Warrenpoint

NEWRY EDWARD STREET

The line which took trains from Goraghwood into the heart of Newry, and Edward Street station, was opened by the Newry and Enniskillen (later renamed Newry and Armagh) Railway in 1854. Railcar 104, which we previously saw at Goraghwood (the junction with the main line), was the mainstay of services over the branch in the 1960s and is seen here in Platform 1. The lattice girders spanning the tracks meant that the platforms could be kept clear of canopy supports; a similar arrangement was used at Armagh. Beyond the canopy we can just glimpse the covered footbridge and Newry South cabin, both very much standard GNR(I) structures. Newry had, at one time, the third busiest goods yard after Dublin and Belfast. The town also had quite an extensive railway system. The Dundalk, Newry and Greenore opened its Bridge Street station in 1873, and then there was the Bessbrook and Newry electric tramway which had its terminus to the right of the photographer.

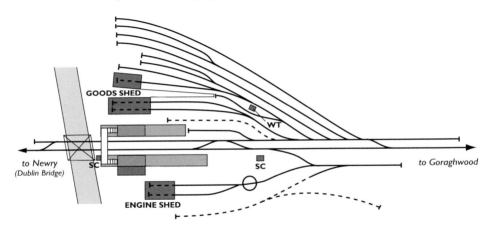

Over on Platform 2 this sign optimistically told passengers that they could get a train to Armagh from here! Passenger services were withdrawn between Goraghwood and Armagh in 1933, and Armagh lost the last of its rail services in 1957. As the service beyond Newry to Warrenpoint was very limited in UTA days, especially during winter, Platform 1 was also often used for departures to Goraghwood. It is interesting to note the British Rail poster to the left, promoting the West Highland line in Scotland, and that the boards still carry the initials 'LMS' 15 years after that company had been nationalised. The site of the station is now occupied by the bus depot.

NEWRY DUBLIN BRIDGE

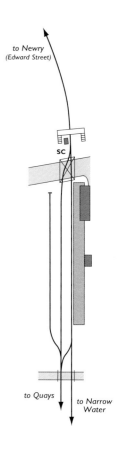

to Newry
(Edward Street)

SC

to Quays

to Narrow
Water

The Newry, Warrenpoint and Rostrevor Railway opened as an isolated line in 1849. Connection with Newry Edward Street (which did not open for another five years) and the rest of the Irish railway network was not made until 1861, when the Town of Newry Connecting Railway provided the link across the Newry Canal. The company's original terminus at Kilmorey Street was replaced by Dublin Bridge at this time. Trains from Warrenpoint to Newry Edward Street ran from left to right.

RF Whitford

The station was on a cramped site. It was built partly over the Clanrye River and comprised a single platform, as this view looking towards Warrenpoint shows. It lost its metal platform roof during a storm a month before opening! The GNR(I) proposed to close Dublin Bridge and concentrate all passenger services at Edward Street, but this idea was abandoned in the face of local opposition. Nowadays there are few traces of the station; it is a vacant site, although some nearby fences are made out of sleepers.

RF Whitford

NARROW WATER

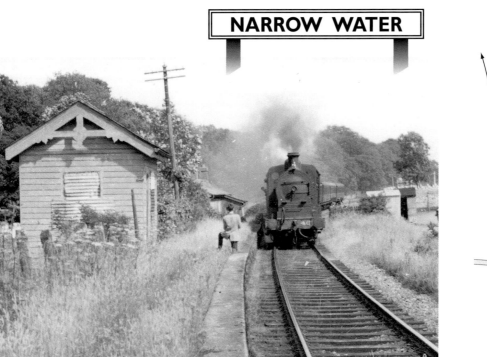

to Newry
(Dublin Bridge)

to Warrenpoint

For much of the section from Newry to Warrenpoint the railway ran along the northern bank of Carlingford Lough, past Narrow Water Castle. Here the NWRR built a halt, consisting of a single platform with this simple wooden building on the down side. The lough and castle are to the right of the photograph. In this 1962 view, No 45 (ex-GNR(I) UG class 0-6-0 No 78) passes with a summer afternoon Belfast-bound train. The halt had closed a few years earlier. The railway at this point, including the site of Narrow Water halt, has been obliterated by the dual carriageway

DJA Young

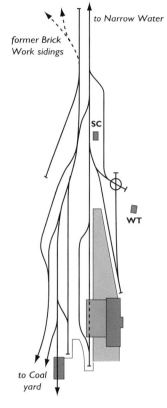

to Narrow Water

former Brick
Work sidings

SC

WT

to Coal
yard

As a port, Warrenpoint was not, in those days, as important as Newry. It also had to compete with Greenore on the other side of Carlingford Lough, from where cross-channel passenger steamers sailed to England. Nevertheless, it was a popular destination for excursion trains, heavily promoted by the GNR(I), and its original, basic, station was replaced by this typical Mills building in 1891.

Despite its title, the Newry, Warrenpoint and Rostrevor Railway never reached Rostrevor. So Warrenpoint station was always a terminus, although between 1877 and 1915 the journey could be completed by horse tram. The GNR(I) provided one main platform, partly covered by an overall roof, and a bay platform. The horse trams departed from under a canopy situated just beyond the station building; the canopy survived some 50 years longer than the trams. Today the station site is used by the Warrenpoint Port Authority and a factory.

The line to Newry and Warrenpoint closed to all traffic in 1965. Surprisingly when the Newry bypass was built, 30 years later, a bridge over the disused track formation was included. Perhaps one day trains might again run at least as far as Newry.

3 The 'Derry Road'

Returning to Portadown, we embark on our journey along the 'Derry Road'. Leaving the main line at Portadown Junction, the first section of this route to Londonderry was opened by the Portadown and Dungannon Railway in 1858. The line was worked and later absorbed by the Ulster Railway, subsequently becoming part of the GNR(I). It was doubled as far as Trew and Moy at the turn of the century but singled, using the up line, in 1960. When these photographs were taken in the early 1960s the line was in its twilight years.

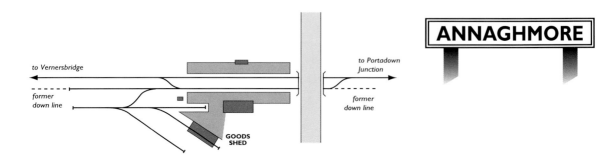

Annaghmore, the first stop, was a delightful country station where the main building resembled a large farmhouse. It was, as we shall see, typical of many provided along the line. Situated in the heart of the 'Orchard County', Annaghmore was the GNR(I)'s principal fruit station.

Opposite top: Looking towards Dungannon, the original PDR building, GNR(I)-built signal cabin and goods sidings were on the down side; the crane can be seen on the beach. A large store was provided specially for the fruit traffic. One of the ubiquitous GNR(I) wooden shelters served the up (Portadown-bound) platform. Only the main building survives today, in use as offices for Francis Neill Insurance Consultants. The goods yard, platform area and forecourt have been levelled off and new showrooms erected for Francis Neill Motors.

VERNERSBRIDGE

Next we reach Venersbridge, closed in 1954. An AEC railcar is passing en route to Londonderry; 20 of these power cars were built for the GNR(I) by AEC Ltd of Southall and introduced to service in 1950. They usually operated in pairs with a non-powered intermediate trailer. The platform area has since been filled in and a large shed built where the photographer is standing.

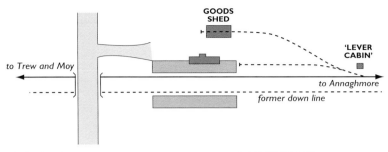

GOODS
SHED

'LEVER
CABIN'

to Trew and Moy

to Annaghmore

former down line

The single-storey station building (on the up side) is now a private residence and beautifully restored. The station never had a signal cabin; the points and signals were controlled by a ground-frame housed in what the GNR(I) called the 'lever cabin'. This view shows the exterior of the building. The provision of this station was influenced by William Verner, a local landowner, and its style was quite different to other buildings on the line. It was approached by a lane from the road which crossed over the line by a bridge, still extant, hence the station's name. The goods shed was to the left of the photographer and still stands.

As the plaque on the gable shows, the station dates from 1862.

A.D
1862

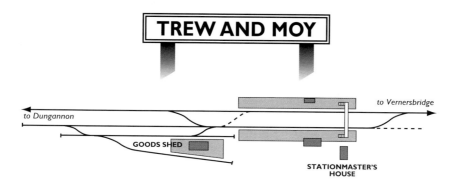

TREW AND MOY

to Vernersbridge

to Dungannon

GOODS SHED

STATIONMASTER'S
HOUSE

Local legend has it that Trew and Moy station was originally called Moy, but that a passenger who alighted and found it some miles from the village sued the railway company. The railway's response was to add the name 'Trew', the townland in which the station stood. Whatever the truth, railwaymen usually referred to it as 'The Moy' and, despite its remoteness from the village, there was a steady movement in livestock through the station. The Moy Fair was one of the largest horse fairs in Ireland. Many of the animals were bought by European buyers and all exports went by rail. In this photograph, No 60 *Slieve Donard* (ex-GNR(I) S class 4-4-0 No 172) arrives from Portadown.

Above: The main building is similar to that at Annaghmore and is also sited on the down platform. Large quantities of mushrooms were transported by rail from Trew and Moy, and indeed the cart on the platform contains mushrooms ready for dispatch. The last stationmaster was Mr Kevin Hughes, and he established K Hughes & Co Mushrooms which now occupies the site. This building now houses the company's main offices. The rest of the station area has been levelled for lorry parking. A standard GNR(I) stationmaster's house can be glimpsed to the right of the footbridge. It is now a private residence for a member of the Hughes family.

Right: On the opposite platform stood one of the traditional wooden shelters. It survives, but on a new site across the former trackbed, beside the stationmaster's house. It is now flanked by a pair of well-maintained GNR(I) signals.

A short distance to the Dungannon side of the station was the goods yard. This picturesque stone goods shed has recently been superbly restored as the canteen for Hughes' Mushrooms' staff. The photograph also shows the crane on the goods beach; unfortunately it is one feature which has not survived.

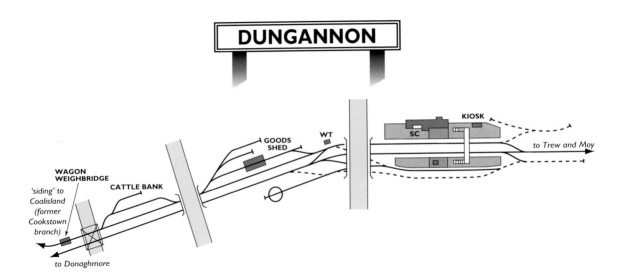

DUNGANNON

WAGON WEIGHBRIDGE

'siding' to Coalisland (former Cookstown branch)

to Donaghmore

CATTLE BANK

GOODS SHED

WT

SC

KIOSK

to Trew and Moy

In contrast to the previous three stations, little of railway interest survives in Dungannon. The original 1858 station was a mile nearer Portadown but three years later, after the tunnel was built, this station opened. Since closure this delightful stone building, surprisingly smaller than most of the company's other station buildings, and all beyond it has been wiped out. The trackbed through the town has been redeveloped as a linear park.

Popping into the general waiting room for a moment, we can view this fine fireplace, complete with an Ulster Railway Company fender of which one or two survive in private collections.

As the railway at Dungannon was at a slightly lower level than the road, and the station building was at road level, these steps under the canopy led from the booking hall and waiting room onto the platform.

On the stone wall, outside the Gents, was a drinking-water fountain, a feature of many stations. This one encouraged users to "Keep the pavement dry"!

Here, an AEC railcar (with power car 119 at the rear) sits in the up platform with a Belfast-bound train. The large volume of traffic from Dungannon, both passenger and goods, also justified local workings to Portadown.

The signal cabin was a variation of the GNR(I) standard, having a wooden base, while the footbridge, now minus its roof, was typical of those we saw on the main line.

Above: Further along the up platform, and just beyond the footbridge, was this unusual but interesting bookstall, disused but still well maintained.

Above right: Across the footbridge was the island platform. Although Dungannon was originally intended to be the end of the line, the PDR later became the Portadown, Dungannon and Omagh Junction Railway Company, and opened its extension to the latter town in 1861. Dungannon then became a junction station in 1879 with the construction of the branch to Cookstown. The nearer face of the island platform served Derry-bound trains whilst the far side served local trains and the former Cookstown branch. The buildings on the island platform were once more extensive than illustrated here.

The branch to Cookstown left the Derry Road at Dungannon Junction, about half a mile beyond the town's station. The track to here was double until October 1959 when the junction was moved back to Dungannon station. The former down line then became the single track for the Derry Road and the former up line became the branch. This allowed the closure of Dungannon Junction cabin and the removal of the signals.

This view is taken from the footplate of No 99 *King George VI*, an ex-NCC W class 2-6-0 'Mogul' on an empty carriages working to Omagh in 1964; the branch is on the right. The cabin stood between these lines, where the two diverged, and was of the usual GNR(I) style. Dungannon Junction also served as a railcar halt; there were no platforms.
EM Patterson, CP Friel Collection

COALISLAND

Construction of the branch to Cookstown was begun by the Dungannon and Cookstown Railway in 1874, but acquired by the GNR(I) before its opening in 1879. Passenger services were withdrawn in January 1956 and goods services beyond Coalisland, the first station on the branch, ceased in January 1959. However there was sufficient business to warrant the retention of the 5½ mile long section to Coalisland right up until the closure of the Derry Road in January 1965. In the 1960s it was worked as a siding from Dungannon station. Exports were sand, imports being coal and bread; coal from Coalisland was just a temporary affair. The mines, one mile north of the village, were connected to the railway but were only open for a brief period in the 1920s. The other nearby collieries had closed many years earlier. Other traffic included goods to and from the linen mill.

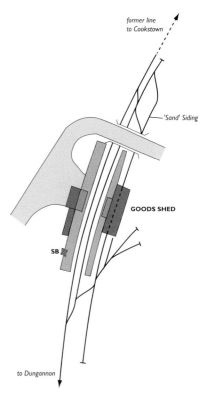

Looking back towards Dungannon Junction we see that the main station building at Coalisland, on the down platform, included both the stationmaster's house and passenger facilities. The signal cabin, which stood beyond it, was blown up by the IRA in June 1957 and rebuilt later that year. Some of these buildings survive in a very derelict condition; the former station site is often occupied by travelling people.

The line served Stewartstown before reaching Cookstown where connection was made with the NCC branch from its Londonderry line.

Stations UK 6132

DONAGHMORE

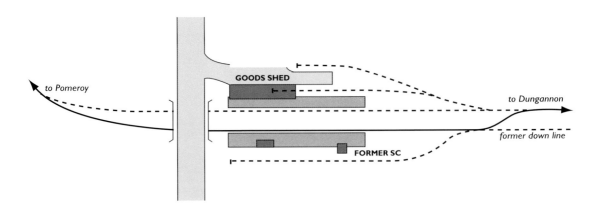

Returning to the Derry Road proper, and the line from Dungannon Junction to Donaghmore was once another section of double track until 1936. This photograph gives all the impressions of a closed station; the usual PDOJR building and adjacent goods store no longer used for railway purposes, and the loop and sidings removed. However, Donaghmore remained open until the end for school traffic, with one request stop in each direction on Mondays to Fridays during term time only. The white patches on the bridge, under which trains to Omagh passed, gave the driver better visibility of the semaphore signals which once stood in front of them. The main station building still stands.

Stations UK 28035

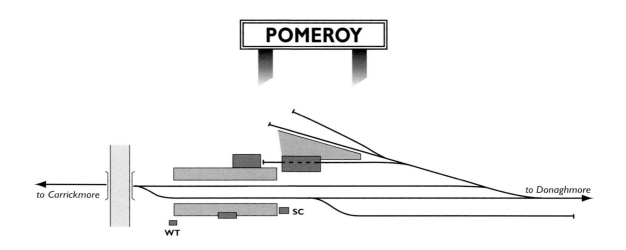

POMEROY

to Carrickmore

to Donaghmore

WT

SC

Right: Pomeroy had the distinction of being the highest mainline station in Ireland. Its main building, on the up platform, was a smaller version of those provided three years earlier at Annaghmore and Trew and Moy. It still featured the simple veranda providing some shelter for passengers, but had gable ends rather than a hipped roof. Just beyond the telegraph pole is the gable wall of the goods shed. It survives, but the area in front of it now serves as the local amenity site.

Left: The shelter on the down platform was rather unusual, with stone walls (which are still standing), slate roof and wooden frontage. The signal cabin was at the Dungannon end of this platform, opposite the goods shed. Milepost 24 (starting from 0 at Portadown Junction), the standard GNR(I) oval, can clearly be seen, as can the name totem below the lamp. One of the noticeboards carries the title 'Belfast Steamship Co Ltd'.

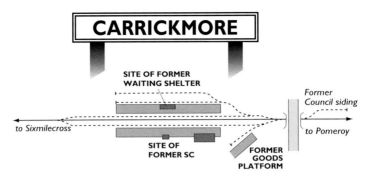

The small station at Carrickmore was situated quite some distance from the town and closed in 1959. The single-storey building still stands, having been used in more recent years for agricultural purposes. However, soon after closure the loop and sidings were lifted and, as the photograph shows, the track realigned. The GNR(I) provided one of their standard signal cabins on the down platform, just beyond the main building, and a wooden shelter on the up side. The goods store once stood on the goods platform to the left. Tyrone County Council had a siding on the Pomeroy side of the overbridge to facilitate the movement of stone from a nearby quarry to other stations in Tyrone and to Co Fermanagh.

Stations UK 28033

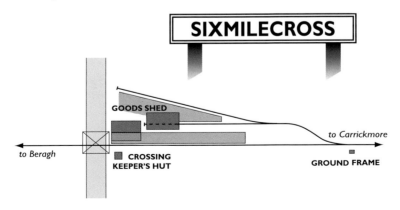

Opened in 1862, a year after the railway itself, was perhaps the most unusual of the stations on this section. It did not have a crossing loop, and the single wooden platform on the up side was built at a later date to the same design as the railmotor halts on the main line. Beyond the stone-built station building, and behind the platform, were two goods sidings. The station was situated beside Sixmilecross and District Co-operative Society's headquarters, and that organisation used the railway for the distribution of bread and other sundries. The canopy on the goods store enabled wagons to be loaded under cover with their produce. There are now few traces of this station.

Stations UK 28031

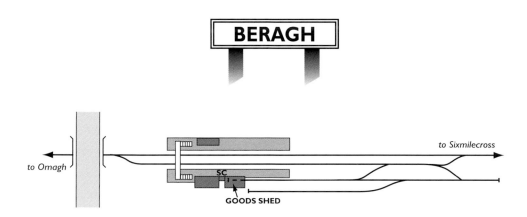

This photograph gives us a good look at the front of the station and goods shed, a view which has changed little over the years. The trains may have gone, the tracks lifted and the platforms filled in, but Beragh station is beautifully maintained and completely intact, including the cabin.

Opposite top: At first glance Beragh seems to have been a rather unusual-looking station. Not so! The main building, on the down platform, was another Trew and Moy/Annaghmore look-alike, with a variation of the GNR(I) signal cabin squeezed in between it and the goods shed, giving the very compact and rather odd appearance. The cabin did not have direct access to the platform, its entrance being to the rear. A footbridge led to the up platform on which was located a large wooden shelter.

OMAGH

to Newtownstewart

SC

GOODS STORE

SC

former line to Enniskillen

to Beragh

ENGINE SHED

Omagh was connected to Derry by rail nine years before the line was completed from Dungannon; the Londonderry and Enniskillen Railway reached the market town in 1852. The LER was later leased to the Dundalk and Enniskillen Railway. The DER became the Irish North Western Railway in 1862 and was absorbed by the GNR(I) in 1883.

It was the INWR which, in 1863, built this imposing building as the town's second station, situated at the junction between the LER and the PDOJR. (The original LER station was about a quarter of a mile closer to Derry.) The canopy is obviously a GNR(I) addition and the chimneys have been rebuilt, at some stage, in yellow brick.

There was a large goods depot here at the station, which was located on the outskirts of the town, but a second depot was more conveniently situated to the town centre. It was served by the 1½-mile-long Market Branch and there were regular local workings between the two depots. Scott animal feeds made considerable use of the goods facilities alongside the passenger station and had their own fleet of wagons. Being a garrison town, military personnel travelling to and from Omagh, in the days before the Troubles, boosted passenger traffic.

Left: On entering the up platform from the main building, past the ticket collector, passengers could buy their daily paper at this atmospheric and well-stocked Eason kiosk.

Opposite top: Here is another view of the up platform showing the canopy which, like that over the entrance, was a later addition. The far section has wooden edging whilst that nearest the photographer has been replaced with corrugated asbestos sheeting. For many years this was the only platform at Omagh, despite it being a junction station, and consequently it was the longest on the GNR(I) system. In fact, the junction was about halfway along the platform, which meant that in the early years trains often sat facing each other as at Limerick Junction.
The standard pattern of covered footbridge was to the left-hand end of the canopy.

Looking along the up platform, on which there is much evidence of parcel traffic, towards Dungannon, we can see the junction between the PDOJR and the LER. The left-hand line is that from Dungannon whilst the storage sidings to the right once led to Enniskillen. In between the two lines is Omagh South cabin.
The sign for the refreshment room is also clearly visible. Inside the room was a sign proclaiming "Service and Civility is our motto". Customers were often greeted with the vernacular version "What d'yis want?"!

Below: On the down side the GNR(I) built a second platform complete with substantial wooden building and canopy. The sign informed passengers bound for Enniskillen, Fintona and Bundoran that they had to complete their journey by bus; that line closed in 1957. There were also two bay platforms to the rear of the main ones, one at each end of the station, but they were little used in later years.

Today it is still possible to travel over the route of the Derry Road through Omagh; the track bed is used as a bypass which obliterates the station. It is known, appropriately, as the Great Northern Road. Just beyond Omagh was the first of two Nestlés factories, both of which were rail connected.

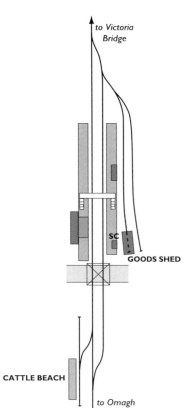

to Victoria
Bridge

SC

GOODS SHED

CATTLE BEACH

to Omagh

NEWTOWNSTEWART

Half a mile outside Newtownstewart, and on the far bank of the river, was the station. The LER was not one of Ireland's wealthier railway companies, and this was reflected in its station buildings which were of a basic wooden construction. Some were replaced by the INWR but many others, including Newtownstewart, were rebuilt by the GNR(I) as soon as they acquired the line.

Opposite bottom: Situated on the down platform the main building was the first along the Derry Road to be constructed in Mills' traditional style of yellow brick, lined with courses of black, brown and purple.

Across the line was the signal cabin and, beyond the footbridge, another of the standard wooden shelters, all forming a very pleasant country station. The Abercorns have their family seat at Baronscourt near Newtownstewart, so royalty often used the station, particularly when the Duke of Abercorn was Governor of Northern Ireland.

In recent years the goods shed was utilised by the Department of Regional Development Roads Service but was demolished in 2001 to make way for a new road; part of it can just be seen behind the cabin.

RF Whitford

VICTORIA BRIDGE

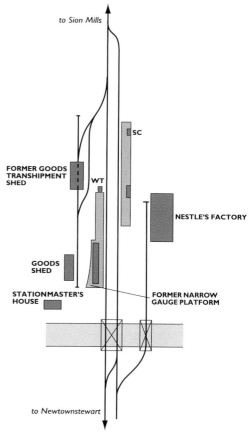

Victoria Bridge was provided with this attractive, and unmistakably GNR(I), station building on the down platform. Built of wood, and similar to those we have already seen at Adelaide and Omagh, it was well maintained by the UTA. Note the cast-iron light standards which have been modified to carry an electric light, and once again station nameplates have been fitted below each of them.

Left: On the up side was an equally attractive wooden signal-cabin which was not of the usual pattern. The station name board stated "Victoria Bridge change for Castlederg." It was from here that passengers could, at one time, change to the Castlederg and Victoria Bridge narrow gauge tramway.

Below: Trains approaching Victoria Bridge from Omagh passed though these level-crossing gates to enter the station. In the background is the second, smaller, Nestlés factory. The building now houses small business units. The up starter-signal post is the creosoted round 'telegraph pole' type, a fairly common feature on the GNR(I).

The roadside tramway ran from 1884 to 1933 and started from the short platform to the rear of the main building; Castelderg is away to our right. To the right of the goods shed we can glimpse the back of the stationmaster's house, built in the GNR(I)'s usual style. It was badly damaged by a bomb in 1972 but repaired and is now the only railway building still extant.

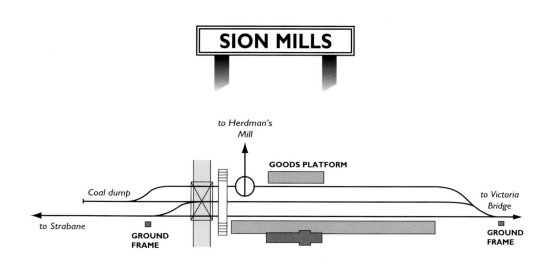

In 1883 the GNR(I) provided Sion Mills with this neat station building, another replacement for an LER structure. Once again Mills was the architect and his design certainly complimented the buildings in the picturesque model village. Indeed, during both GNR(I) and UTA days Sion Mills station regularly came top in its class in the 'Best Kept Station' competition. This view shows the approach from the village to the station house. Built in yellow brick and again relieved by black, brown and purple brick courses, it was unusual for the GNR(I) in that the stationmaster's accommodation was incorporated into the main building alongside the facilities for passengers.

There was only one platform at Sion Mills, on the down side. Although the goods yard comprised two loops, they were usually filled with wagons which meant that local goods workings, and the daily steam-hauled passenger train which brought mill workers from Strabane, had to work in push-pull fashion. The locomotive propelled its train in the down direction. Part of the platform face survives but, sadly, nothing else. Much of the area is now given over to a car park serving the 'Riverside Walk'.

The 'Mills' in Sion Mills refers to the Herdman's flax spinning mill. Wagons were hauled by tractor from the mill, seen in the background, onto a wagon turntable on the loop furthest from the station platform. The old mill building currently lies empty but Herdmans is very much in business, operating from a more recent building alongside the former station.

STRABANE

The railway from Londonderry reached Strabane in 1847. It eventually became one of the most important railway centres in Northern Ireland – it was a UK customs post and the interchange with the narrow gauge County Donegal Railway (jointly owned by the GNR(I) and the LMS). Yet today there is little to show that railways ever ran through Strabane. The GNR(I) station building dated from the takcover of the INWR and, once again, was unmistakably built in Mills style but this time in red brick lined with yellow and black. It was on the up platform. The GNR(I) provided the CDRJC with their own station building on the far side of the complex. It was built in similar style, but in yellow brick, and housed the refreshment rooms.

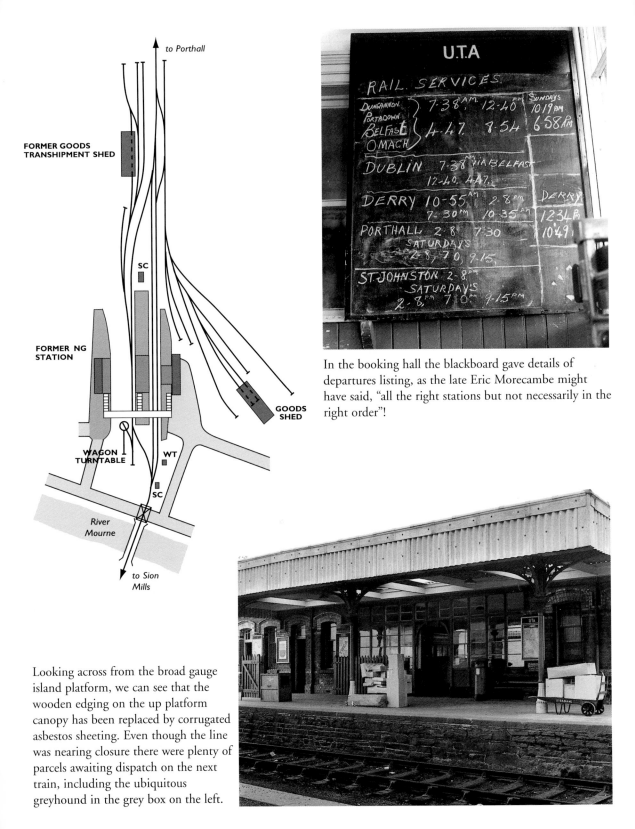

FORMER GOODS
TRANSHIPMENT SHED

to Porthall

SC

FORMER NG
STATION

WAGON
TURNTABLE

WT

SC

GOODS
SHED

River
Mourne

to Sion
Mills

In the booking hall the blackboard gave details of departures listing, as the late Eric Morecambe might have said, "all the right stations but not necessarily in the right order"!

Looking across from the broad gauge island platform, we can see that the wooden edging on the up platform canopy has been replaced by corrugated asbestos sheeting. Even though the line was nearing closure there were plenty of parcels awaiting dispatch on the next train, including the ubiquitous greyhound in the grey box on the left.

Here is one of the nameboards which advised passengers that they could change to the CDRJC, and even continue their journey beyond Letterkenny by the Londonderry and Lough Swilly Railway. However, the last narrow gauge trains ran on New Year's Eve 1959, so by the time these pictures were taken journeys into Co Donegal had to be made by road. The CDRJC provided the replacement buses and continued to use their station as the bus depot. One of these nameboards is on display in the rail gallery at the Ulster Folk and Transport Museum, Cultra.

CIÉ handled a lot of goods traffic to and from the Derry Road, hence the wagon with the 'Flying Snail' logo. Often these were from one station in Éire, through Northern Ireland, and on to another in Éire, in which case the wagons were fitted with customs seals. They were known by railwaymen, right up until closure of the line, as 'Free to Free wagons' even though the name 'Irish Free State' effectively disappeared in 1937.

This photograph of the island platform, looking north towards Londonderry, gives us a good view of the canopy structure. The GNR(I) manufactured the metalwork for its canopies and footbridges at its Dundalk works. The CDRJC narrow gauge station was to the left of the picture.

At the end of the island platform was Strabane North cabin; it can be seen in the distance in the previous photograph. The down starter signal post is another of those mounted on a round post.

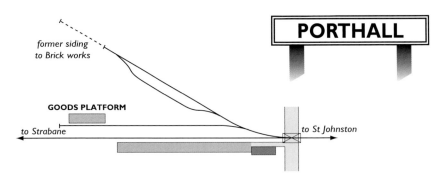

PORTHALL

former siding to Brick works

GOODS PLATFORM

to Strabane

to St Johnston

Beyond Strabane the railway crossed the River Foyle and the border into Co Donegal. There the stations were owned and manned by Éire's transport operator, CIÉ, although the passenger services were run by the UTA. Each of the stations on this section, the first being Porthall, also featured an Irish customs post.

Porthall, opened in 1848, had a single platform and some goods sidings, one of which led to a brick works. The GNR(I) later provided this main building, similar in style to those at Balmoral and between Lisburn and Antrim. It remained open until the end and, despite being nowhere near a town or village, enjoyed a reasonable amount of passenger and goods traffic as there was no bus service in the vicinity then. The platform and goods dock are still there.

Stations UK 27930

ST JOHNSTON

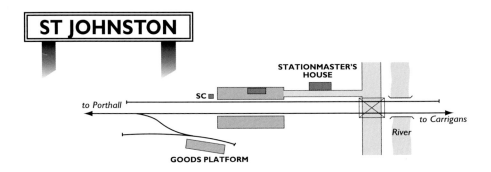

STATIONMASTER'S HOUSE

SC

to Porthall

to Carrigans

River

GOODS PLATFORM

St Johnston was the last major station in Co Donegal and the destination of many of the sealed goods vehicles which started their journey in Éire and arrived here via Northern Ireland. It was also the only crossing place between Strabane and Londonderry. St Johnston opened in 1847 and was later provided with a building which was similar to that at Porthall, but this time on the down platform. There was a signal cabin beyond it and on the opposite platform a wooden shelter. We can also see, to the right, part of the stationmaster's house. Both it and the main building survive as private dwellings; the latter is now rendered but still clearly stands on the platform.

Stations UK 27929

CARRIGANS

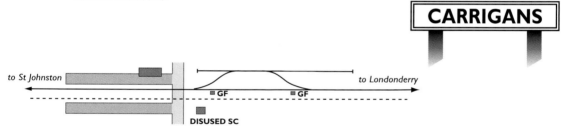

The line from St Johnston to Londonderry was double until 1932, the only intermediate station being Carrigans which also opened in 1847. Here, the building on the down side was replaced with this concrete structure which included the customs hall. It has since been extended and altered to become another private residence. Goods facilities were provided slightly further down the line, behind the photographer. The goods platform and base of the signal cabin can still be seen.

Stations UK 27928

From Carrigans the railway followed the bank of the River Foyle and crossed the border once again to re-enter Northern Ireland before reaching its terminus in Londonderry.

Foyle Road station was built for the INWR to an Italianate design by Thomas Turner, replacing the earlier LER facility. It had the advantage over its NCC rival in being on the cityside of the river, whereas the Northern Counties trains ran to Waterside station directly across the River Foyle. However, its big disadvantage was the longer distance from Belfast to Derry on the GNR(I), particularly after the NCC opened the Bleach Green loop line in 1934.

Opposite: Foyle Road had a neat and well-maintained concourse which was remodelled by the GNR(I) in 1899. A feature was the company's monograms in the stained glass of the doors which once led to the refreshment rooms and the stationmaster's office. In the archway, above the seat, is one of the three war memorials erected by the GNR(I) after the First World War, the others being at its termini in Belfast and Dublin. The Derry memorial was put into storage when the station closed, but around ten years later the crest and some letters from it were used to repair that from Great Victoria Street. It had been damaged in a bomb explosion and underwent restoration before being put on display, together with the BCDR memorial from Belfast Queen's Quay, in Belfast Central in 1976. In 1993 I asked Don Price, then Managing Director of NIR, if the Foyle Road memorial could be put back on display as part of that year's commemorative events marking the 75th anniversary of the armistice. Work was started on its restoration with a view to erecting it alongside the others in Belfast Central, but it was then discovered that it carried the same names as those erected in Belfast and Dublin.

The concourse was once well decorated with hanging baskets.

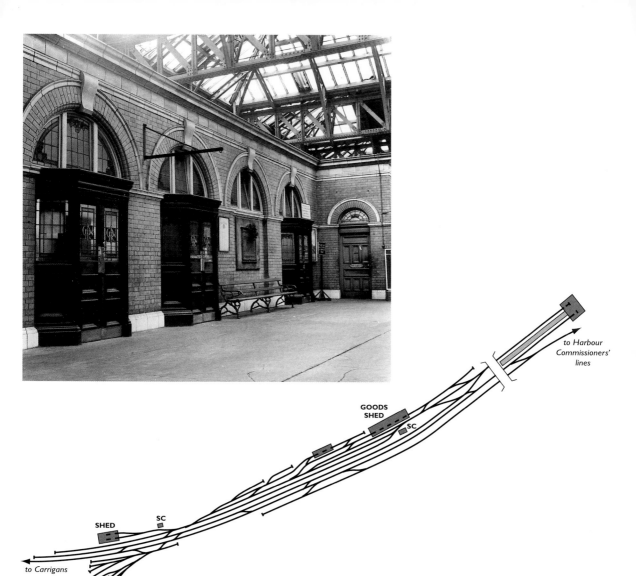

to Harbour
Commissioners'
lines

GOODS
SHED

SC

SHED

SC

to Carrigans

WT   ENGINE SHED

Right top: These timetables and information boards were on the platform barrier. Only one more timetable was issued for the Derry Road. In January 1965 the line closed and soon the tracks were lifted. The station was demolished in 1970.

Right bottom: Passenger trains arrived and departed from an island platform. The pillars supporting the canopy also included GNR(I) monograms, being of the same pattern as those we saw at Great Victoria Street, Lisburn and Lurgan. Foyle Road was the only station on the Derry Road to have them.

Looking out from the concourse, Craigavon Bridge is in the background. The lower deck of the bridge used to have mixed 5'3" and 3'0" gauge track to link Londonderry's four termini. (The narrow gauge stations at Victoria Road and Pennyburn had long since closed.)

The narrow gauge Foyle Valley Railway and Museum is now based on the track bed of the Derry Road, on the far side of the Craigavon Bridge.

4 The Antrim Branch

Although the branch line from Knockmore Junction to Antrim lost its regular passenger service in 1960, it remained open for goods traffic and stock transfers between the former GNR(I) and NCC lines. Indeed its importance as a goods line grew in 1965 with the closure of the Derry Road. CIÉ goods services between Éire and Londonderry were then diverted via the branch and the NCC main line. The Antrim branch was also used for special passenger workings such as Sunday school excursions and enthusiasts' trains. Regular passenger services were restored by NIR in 1974, and between 1978 and 2001 mainline trains between Belfast and Londonderry used this route to Belfast instead of the NCC line from Antrim to Bleach Green.

The line was opened in 1871 by the grandly-titled Dublin and Antrim Junction Railway, although the junction at Knockmore always faced Belfast, not Dublin. From the outset it was leased and worked by the UR, but in 1879 was bought by the UR's successor, the GNR(I), who upgraded the stations along the route in a common style of red brick with yellow and black brick ornamental courses.

Railway convention suggests that the 'up' direction is the one in which trains travel when going towards the company's main station; Dublin in the GNR(I)'s case. However, on the Antrim branch that convention was reversed, trains to Antrim being regarded as 'up' trains, so that is the definition of 'up' and 'down' used in this chapter. (It is only in NIR times that Antrim-bound trains have been referred to as 'down' trains.).

Previous page: The first stop was at Brookmount which, like most stations on the line, opened in 1871 and lasted until the UTA's withdrawal of passenger services. There was a single passenger platform, on the down side, on which the station building stood. The overgrown track on the left was the goods loop which served a cattle dock and platform from which lime was loaded onto wagons. The main building was demolished many years ago but the platform and stationmaster's house behind are extant.

The locomotive at the head of this Junior Orange Order 'special' is UTA No 43, formerly GNR(I) SG class 0-6-0 No 175.

AR Donaldson, courtesy WT Scott

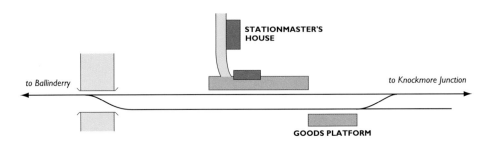

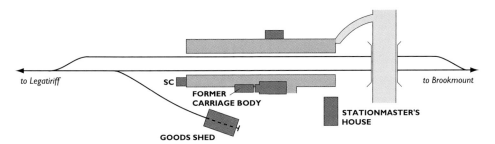

Opposite: Two halts were passed before reaching Ballinderry. Brookhill opened in 1933 and gained a platform three years later; it can still be seen on the up side. Meeting House opened in 1939 but never had a platform; instead, steps were put against the carriages to let passengers embark and alight.

Ballinderry was the first crossing point on the branch and was given a larger version of the station building provided at Brookmount. It was built on the up platform, the station being completed by the usual style of wooden shelter, on the down side, and signal cabin. A grounded coach body provided extra storage. When the station reopened in 1974, the main building was retained but adapted to become an open shelter. It also housed the new signalling equipment which allowed the loop to be worked from Antrim.

The goods yard was behind the cabin. The remains of the goods shed and platform survive, as does the stationmaster's house, but the down-side shelter and signal cabin have gone.

EM Patterson, CP Friel collection

Legatiriff Halt opened in 1936 and, as we can see in this view, was another halt without a platform. Only the most basic facilities were provided – an old goods van and a redundant passenger carriage serving as the station buildings. Ex-NCC 'Jeep' No 55 is hauling an Orangemen's special to Ballinderry on 12 July 1965.

Craig Robb

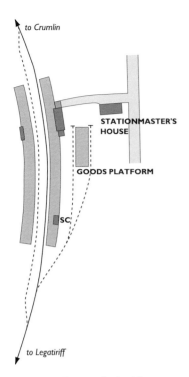

to Crumlin

STATIONMASTER'S HOUSE

GOODS PLATFORM

SC

to Legatiriff

GLENAVY

Right top: At Glenavy the building was on the down side. By the 1960s the good yard, reputed to have had one of the sharpest curves on the Irish broad gauge, and passing loop had been lifted. When the line was upgraded in the 1970s, the track through the station and the down platform face were realigned leaving insufficient clearance for a second track. The remains of the up platform are still there. As at Ballinderry, the glass screen was removed to create an open shelter prior to Glenavy reopening in 1974. By 2001 the building was heavily vandalised and demolished. The former stationmaster's house, at the far end of the access road to the station, is another private residence.

Right bottom: Further along the down platform, at the Lisburn end, was this very fine example of the company's signal cabins. The box with the 'T' on it contained a telephone for use, after the cabin and loop closed, at busy times when temporary sections were introduced to handle additional traffic, usually on big Loyal Orders' days.

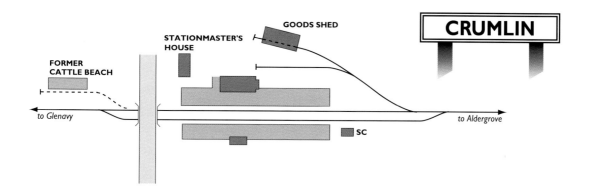

Crumlin was very similar to Ballinderry – an over bridge at the Lisburn end, two platforms, an identical main station building on the up side, wooden shelter on the down, and a goods yard behind the up platform. One difference was the position of the cabin, at the Antrim end of the up platform. Crumlin has always been one of the busiest stations on the branch and when this photograph was taken, shortly before closure to regular passenger services, there was a large batch of parcels sitting on the up platform awaiting dispatch. At the bottom of the down platform ramp, nearest the camera, is a permanent-way trolley with flanged wheels.

Once again only the main building lasted for the reopening in 1974, serving as a shelter and housing the signalling equipment. Crumlin became the second passing point on the branch.

More recently, part of the main building has been replaced by a metal shelter, although the portion housing the signalling equipment still stands. The remains of the goods building can still be seen. In the late 1970s a siding was reinstated here to assist in the disposal of withdrawn railcars. They were lined with blue asbestos and could not be scrapped. Instead, they were loaded onto lorries and brought to a nearby disused quarry and drowned.

Soon after leaving Crumlin, trains cross an attractive girder bridge, the main civil engineering feature on the branch. Just beyond it a siding once served the linen mill.

EM Patterson, CP Friel collection

ALDERGROVE

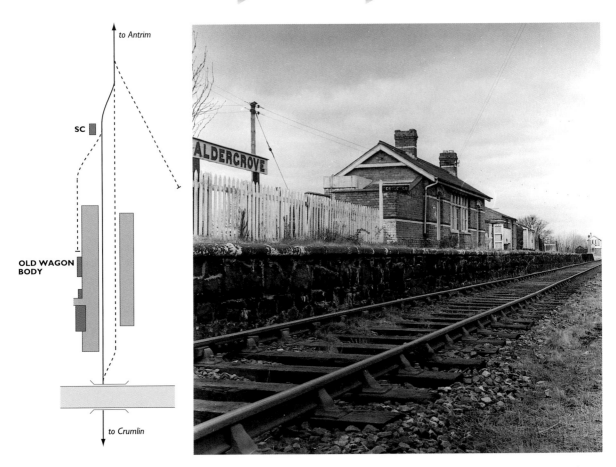

A mile beyond Crumlin was a junction with a 2¼-mile-long siding to Gortnagallon, a wartime aircraft factory. Both goods and passenger trains operated over the 'siding' which was in use from 1942 until 1945, and resulted in a considerable increase in traffic over the branch. One and a quarter miles further on was Aldergrove station. Aldergrove had one of the smaller buildings, similar in size but not identical to Brookmount, which stood on the up side. The volume of traffic on the branch during the Second World War led to the construction of a passing loop, down platform and signal cabin in 1942.

Prior to 1960, there were local workings to Aldergrove from Ballymena and Antrim to bring workers to the nearby RAF base. Indeed, the railway played a role in the early development of the aerodrome; a siding was opened in 1916 to assist in its construction. It was three miles long and diverged from the branch via a facing junction (travelling from Aldergrove to Antrim) which was about 250 yards beyond the platforms. It was last used in 1945. For some years there have been suggestions that some arrangement should be made for trains on the branch to serve the nearby Belfast International Airport. The railway runs alongside the airport perimeter, but this would require the construction of a spur or diversion of the entire line. From Aldergrove the line continues for another 5¼ miles, past the site of Millar's Bridge Halt (opened in 1938, and another halt which never had a platform), before entering the NCC station at Antrim. (Antrim is featured in the next chapter.)

5 The NCC Main Line: Belfast to Portrush

In April 1848 the Belfast and Ballymena Railway opened and with it Belfast's second terminus. (The BBR was renamed Belfast and Northern Counties Railway in 1860.) Sadly, much of York Road station was destroyed during the Blitz of 1941, so to appreciate its appearance in the 1960s it is worth looking at a much earlier photograph, taken in 1937.

The original building was designed by the renowned Belfast architect Sir Charles Lanyon in classical style. There was a grand two-storey entrance block flanked by two wings. This backed onto a single platform; alongside the platform track were some storage sidings and a goods platform beyond. This was covered by an overall roof.

Expansion of the station was deferred, as the proposed Belfast Central Railway would have created one terminus for all rail services in the city, but in 1873 the BNCR built a goods shed and the former goods platform became a second passenger platform.

In 1894 further alterations were completed under the guidance of Berkeley Deane Wise. He joined the company from the Belfast and Co Down Railway in 1888 and over the next 18 years, until his retirement due to ill health, he exerted a great influence on BNCR architecture, just as William Henry Mills did on the GNR(I). The clock tower was built together with the adjacent canopy under which tram lines were laid. A few years later some of the sidings between the two platforms were removed and a new island platform provided. A bay platform was also built to the rear of the former goods platform. The Station Hotel, later known as the Midland Hotel, opened in 1898; it was to the right of the photograph.

The BNCR was acquired by the (English) Midland Railway Company in 1903 and run by its 'Northern Counties Committee'. It became part of the London Midland and Scottish Railway in the 'Grouping' of 1923.

Nationalisation in Great Britain meant that, in 1948, the NCC became a region of the Railway Executive of the British Transport Commission, only for it to be absorbed by the UTA the following year.

W Robb

BELFAST YORK ROAD

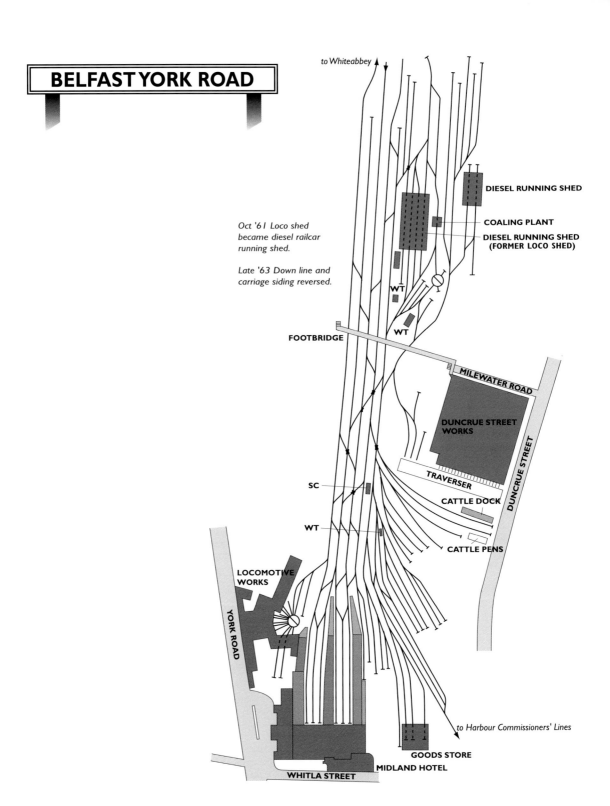

to Whiteabbey

DIESEL RUNNING SHED

COALING PLANT

DIESEL RUNNING SHED
(FORMER LOCO SHED)

Oct '61 Loco shed
became diesel railcar
running shed.

Late '63 Down line and
carriage siding reversed.

WT

WT

FOOTBRIDGE

MILEWATER ROAD

DUNCRUE STREET
WORKS

DUNCRUE STREET

TRAVERSER

SC

CATTLE DOCK

WT

CATTLE PENS

LOCOMOTIVE
WORKS

YORK ROAD

to Harbour Commissioners' Lines

GOODS STORE

MIDLAND HOTEL

WHITLA STREET

As already mentioned, York Road suffered in the German air raids of 1941; Wise's canopy and the hotel were destroyed. This was the main station entrance as it appeared after reconstruction, actually fronting Whitla Street. The hotel, part of which can just be seen to the right of the entrance, was also rebuilt and is the only part of the station standing today. It is now used as an office block and is known as the Midland Building.

Lanyon's grand entrance, which contained the boardroom on the upper floor, was so badly damaged that it had to be quickly demolished by the Royal Engineers; this is all that survived, relegated to the role of parcels loading bay.

The station suffered further bomb damage in the 1970s. With the imminent transfer of Londonderry-line services to Belfast Central, a new, smaller, terminus building was opened in 1975 for the sole use of the Larne line. Its entrance was on roughly the same site as Lanyon's.

York Road was replaced by nearby Yorkgate in 1992 and much of the site used for an expansion of the railway workshops.

Wise remodelled the interior of York Road in a style described by some as Swiss and by others as Norwegian. This kiosk, which once had a clock tower, survived the Blitz. It is now preserved in the rail gallery at the Ulster Folk and Transport Museum where it is used as the Midland Buffet.

The war memorial was erected by the NCC in 1920. When the new terminus building opened in 1975, it was moved to a new location behind the buffer stops. Following the closure of York Road it was moved again, this time to Carrickfergus. The concourse area is now occupied by the Plumb Centre.

Another example of the Swiss/Norwegian chalet style was the booking and enquiry office. The inauguration of Northern Ireland Railways in 1968 was marked by the unveiling of a revamped interior to York Road. This featured a new platform barrier, kiosks and booking office. Wise's booking office, although redundant, was retained, only to be destroyed by a terrorist bomb in 1972.

The twin-arched glass roof, which we saw in the previous two photographs, originally covered the concourse and much of the platforms; however, it was badly damaged in the air raids. Only the portion which covered the concourse was repaired, cantilevered 'umbrella' canopies being provided on the platforms.

This is a view along York Road's original platform, Platform 1, looking away from the concourse. It was removed by NIR in 1969 to make way for a new diesel running shed. The canopy steelwork was reused at Portrush where it still stands. The carriages to the right are in the storage siding between Platforms 1 and 2. There was a similar siding between Platforms 3 and 4. York Road did not have locomotive release roads.

Before leaving York Road, let's take a look at the types of passenger train operating on the former NCC lines in the early 1960s. Although the workshops here, and at nearby Duncrue Street, had pioneered the development of diesel railcars many years earlier, York Road had the distinction of having the last mainline steam shed in the British Isles. The UTA had inherited a fleet of modern Class WT 2-6-4 tank locomotives, popularly known as the 'Jeeps', built by the LMS in Derby in 1946–50 for the NCC. Many lasted into NIR days and hauled service trains until Easter 1970.

This photograph is taken from the signal cabin, looking towards the terminus, and shows 'Jeep' No 2 (built in 1947) departing on a light passenger working. The train is about to pass under a gantry carrying a range of shunting signals. The colour light signalling system was introduced in 1926, the first such installation in

Ireland, and remained in use until 1984 when York Road was resignalled and the cabin closed.

To the left of the train we can see some wagons in the goods yard; nowadays the main running lines to Yorkgate and Belfast Central run through here and along the far side of the Midland Hotel, just visible in the distance. The large building to the right is Associated Feed Manufacturers Ltd, nowadays John Thompson and Sons Ltd animal feeds plant; trains still pass it today.

Steam and diesel operated side by side as this view from the cabin, looking away from the terminus, testifies. Another 'Jeep' is departing on a goods working whilst one of the multi-purpose diesel railcar sets, introduced by the UTA in the late 1950s and headed by power-car 44, is arriving. They were called 'multi-purpose' because they were also used to haul goods trains during off-peak hours when not required for passenger workings. Other diesel-hauled services of the early 1960s were worked by the multi-engined diesel railcars introduced in the early 1950s, primarily for the Bangor line. On the right-hand end of the gantry, which mainly carries another batch of shunting signals, is one of the 1926 vintage two-aspect running signals. Beyond it and the footbridge, we can just glimpse the roof of the engine shed and the concrete coaling tower which dominated this part of the yard. On the left is the former Jennymount Mill, now Jennymount Industrial Estate.

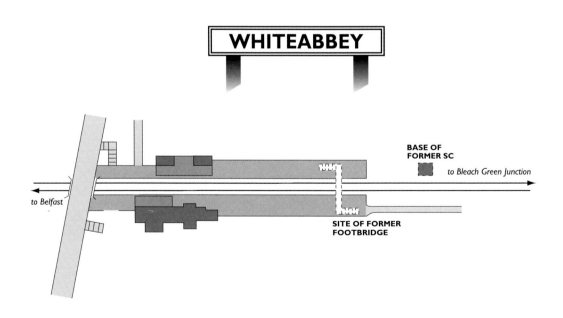

WHITEABBEY

BASE OF
FORMER SC

to Bleach Green Junction

to Belfast

SITE OF FORMER
FOOTBRIDGE

Whiteabbey was the first stop outside Belfast, the intermediate halts at Greencastle and Whitehouse having closed in 1916 and 1954 respectively. (Whitehouse had its brief moment of glory in 1941 when it was used as a temporary terminus following the bombing of York Road.)

The main building at Whiteabbey, on the up (Belfast-bound) platform, was built in 1863; the canopy was added about 50 years later. The building replaced the original structure and survived into the 1980s when it was demolished to make way for a basic shelter. It offered living accommodation for the stationmaster, waiting rooms and booking office.

On the bridge we can see one of the searchlight signals installed as part of the Loop Line scheme in 1934. Unlike conventional colour light signals, which had a separate bulb and coloured lens for each aspect, searchlight signals had just one bulb. The colour was changed by moving pieces of coloured glass, mounted in a 'spectacle', in front of the bulb, this being achieved electromechanically. Also on the bridge, at the end of the platform, is a box with a 'T' on it; the telephone inside enabled the driver of a train halted at a red light to speak to the signalman at Greenisland.

On the down (Portrush/Londonderry-bound) platform this fine, mainly wooden, shelter and waiting rooms were added in the 1890s, another example of Wise's architecture. NIR also replaced it with a small metal shelter. A short steam-hauled passenger train has just departed and is heading towards Bleach Green Junction. The base of the signal cabin can be seen alongside the rear carriage. It closed in 1934 when the searchlight signals were installed.

BLEACH GREEN JUNCTION

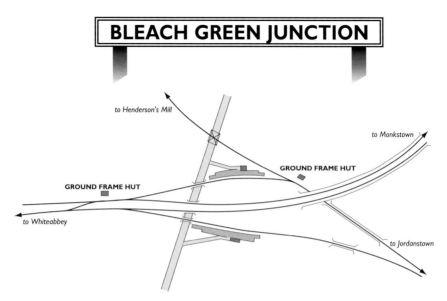

to Henderson's Mill

to Monkstown

GROUND FRAME HUT

GROUND FRAME HUT

to Whiteabbey

to Jordanstown

Below left: For almost 90 years mainline trains ran through to Greenisland. There they changed direction before continuing their journey north. After 60 years in the planning, the NCC opened the loop line on 17 January 1934, construction having started in January 1931. For the first time trains could run directly from York Road to Portrush and Londonderry, diverging from the old route at a new junction – Bleach Green. The new section of main line, which was grant aided by the Northern Ireland government as a job-creation scheme, necessitated the construction of this fine concrete viaduct across Valentine's Glen. It is 630 feet long and 70 feet high. The three main arches each have a span of 89 feet whilst the seven smaller ones each have a span of 35 feet. At the time of building it was the largest reinforced concrete bridge in the British Isles.

The line from Bleach Green Junction to Antrim closed to regular trains in 1978, when they were re-routed into Belfast Central via Lisburn, although a short-lived shuttle service ran over the line from June 1980 to February 1981. Eventually it reopened to regular mainline trains in June 2001 by which time they could access Belfast Central via the Dargan Bridge over the Lagan.

Opposite bottom right: The Larne line diverged from the main line by means of a superbly designed double-track 'burrowing' junction. This meant that at no time did a train have to cross the path of one travelling in the opposite direction. A second, smaller, concrete viaduct was also built to carry the down Larne line over the glen. It is 400 feet long and 40 feet high, the arches having the same spans as those on the mainline viaduct. From the junction the main line climbed to such an extent that down trains to Larne dived under the larger viaduct. Up trains from Larne continued to use the original stone viaduct which ran round the far side of the mainline one. To ease the gradients on the main line, the track levels at Bleach Green Junction were raised. This was achieved on the up Larne line by building a small embankment on top of the earlier viaduct!

The mainline gradients were further eased by lowering the track bed from Monkstown, where the new line met up with the old, to Mossley. The original route between Greenisland and Monkstown was also lowered and reduced to single track. It became known as the 'back line'. In this view, looking north, we see the back line diverging from the new route. This concrete bridge was one of five new bridges built as part of the project and replaced a level crossing. Beyond it is Monkstown halt, opened in 1934 to suit the new alignment and which replaced the 1905 station. It comprised concrete-faced platforms with a basic shelter on each. It had a chequered career, closing in 1959, reopening in 1967 and closing again in 1978. In September 1980, three months after the introduction of the shuttle service, Monkstown reopened once more, but only lasted five months. To the left of the up line is the signal cable. The new cabling for the 1934 installation was suspended on a wire which in turn was supported by a series of short concrete posts, an unusual arrangement as the cabling is normally suspended on telegraph posts, laid in cable ducts or buried underground. Nowadays the double track from Bleach Green Junction becomes single here, but prior to 1986 it was double right through to Ballymena. The platforms were removed in 2000 during reconstruction of the line.

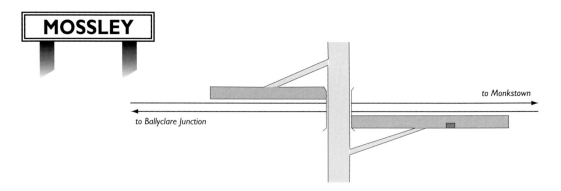

MOSSLEY

to Monkstown

to Ballyclare Junction

This is the point where the new track alignment reached the same level as the original, but Mossley also required a new halt to replace the 1899 structure. The platforms were staggered on either side of another example of the NCC's 1930s concrete bridge architecture; again the bridge was built as part of the loop-line scheme and replaced a level crossing. Mossley closed in 1954 but was back in use from September 1980 to February 1981. The platforms are extant but the bridge has been widened.

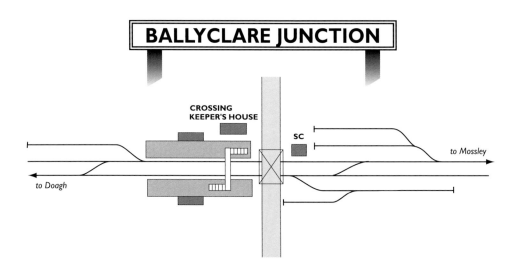

BALLYCLARE JUNCTION

CROSSING
KEEPER'S HOUSE

SC

to Mossley

to Doagh

There was a halt here, known as Ballynure Road, long before the Ballyclare branch opened in 1884. Although the actual junction between the main line and branch was about a mile further north, at Kingsbog Junction, the halt was renamed Ballyclare Junction. It consisted of wooden platforms, each provided with a shelter, alongside the level crossing where the Belfast–Larne road traversed the railway.

The crossing keeper's cottage is seen here behind the up platform; the crossing itself was to the right of it. In front of the cottage was a cast-iron lattice footbridge, removed before this photograph was taken. At the far, Belfast side, of the level crossing was the signal cabin, on the up side, plus some sidings on both sides of the line. In the early 1960s they were used for the storage of surplus and withdrawn carriages.

The level crossing was replaced in 1967 by the bridge which carries the A8 over the railway, and all other traces of this station have also gone.

Passenger services on the Ballyclare branch ended in 1938 and goods traffic in 1950, but Ballyclare Junction station remained open until 1961. Some services from Londonderry divided here, with one portion continuing to Belfast and the other proceeding to Larne Harbour via the 'back line', an arrangement which ended in September 1958.

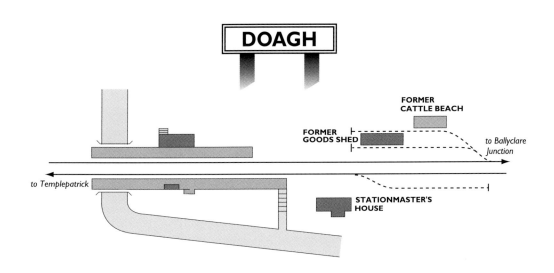

DOAGH

FORMER CATTLE BEACH

FORMER GOODS SHED

to Ballyclare Junction

to Templepatrick

STATIONMASTER'S HOUSE

The long-closed railmotor halt at Ballyrobert is passed before we reach Doagh, one of the original stations on the line. At first it was called Ballypallady, and later Ballyclare and Doagh until the branch to Ballyclare opened. It was rebuilt in 1863 and this new building, in basalt base and red brick upper with yellow brick around the windows and doors, was erected alongside the up platform.

It bears some similarity to Craigavad on the Belfast, Holywood and Bangor Railway which was also built at about the same time, highlighting Sir Charles Lanyon's influence on both companies. Lanyon was consulting engineer to both the BNCR and the BHBR.

This view shows the main building, looking towards Antrim. Across the tracks on the down platform is a store and a prefabricated cast-iron Gents toilet. Doagh closed in 1970 and the main building plus the platforms have gone, although the steps up to both are still there! The stationmaster's house, which was provided on the down side, has survived in private ownership, screened from the railway by a high hedge.

Stations UK 27830

Most stations were individually designed to suit their environment, but they did often feature structures which were of a standard pattern used elsewhere and often bought in from a manufacturer's catalogue. Typical examples were railings, water columns, footbridges and lamp standards. The prefabricated cast-iron Gents on the down platform at Doagh was another example; this one was manufactured by the George Smith Sun Foundry, Alloa.

Wise was a pioneer in the use of concrete, and so it featured widely on the NCC . By 1911 the company had its own casting yard in Belfast where they made a wide range of items including fencing, lamp standards, signal posts, signs and parts for platforms and buildings. An early example of the latter was the goods store at Doagh which dated from 1916.

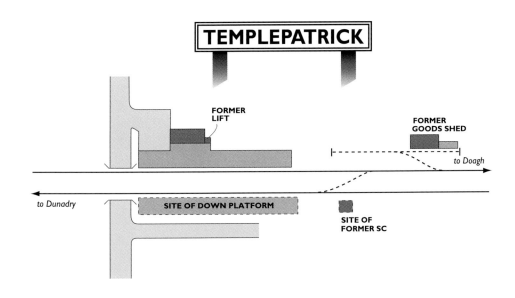

Right: Templepatrick was built high on an embankment, so the main building was another two-storey structure with basalt base and red brick upper with black and yellow ornamental courses. It served the up platform which was accessed by an internal stone staircase. The construction of the platform can clearly be seen, consisting of concrete pillars supporting concrete slabs and therefore erected at a much later date, replacing the wooden structure. Templepatrick closed in 1954 and ceased to be a block post in 1965, but reopened briefly in September 1980. By that time the building and surrounding ground had been sold and the basement was being used as a garage. However, NIR had retained a right of way through the building, so Belfast-bound passengers had to go through the garage to get to the platform!

Below left: Here, looking towards Antrim, we can just glimpse the building behind the bushes. Again we can see the section of platform, in front of the building, which consisted of pillars supporting slabs. That nearest the camera was of a more conventional style, a solid structure with concrete face. The down platform was wooden and has been removed; when the station was in use in 1980–1, a temporary platform was built here.
The station building survives, well maintained in private use; meanwhile there are proposals for a new station at Templepatrick but on another site.

Stations UK 27831

Above: This unusual contraption was a lift used to bring luggage and parcels to and from the platform on the much higher level. It was sited at the Belfast end of the main building.

Continued on page 113

Along the GNR

Belfast Great Victoria Street station was admired by many including the late Poet Laureate and railway enthusiast, Sir John Betjeman. Shown here after refurbishment in 1961–2, the alterations had already spoiled its appearance, particularly the modern bar entrance and the upper storey with square windows built above. The site is now occupied by the Europa Hotel and the Great Northern Mall.

DJA Young

Finaghy Halt, recently repainted, looking towards Belfast on 28 August 1965. Ex-NCC WT class 'Jeep' No 51 is heading for Lisburn with an Orangemen's special. The halt is a good example of those built by the GNR(I) to serve its Belfast commuter trains.

DJA Young

The up platform building at Dunmurry was typical of many of the smaller station buildings provided by the GNR(I) throughout its network. Now cement rendered, it is used by an office supply company.

The impressive facade of Sir John Macneill's building at Portadown was well suited to a station which became known as the 'Hub of the North'. The taller building on the right-hand end was the original 1842 station, later used for many years by the Post Office.　　　　　　　　　　　　　　　　　*RF Whitford*

Portadown had one of the few roundhouses built in Ireland. VS class No 58 *Lagan*, still in GNR(I) livery in 1963, sits outside. She is resting after hauling a goods train on a running-in trip prior to hauling a rugby special from Belfast to Dublin.

Craig Robb

'Jeep' No 51 passes through Poyntzpass with a 13 July special. These trains brought spectators to the Sham Fight at Scarva and then continued to Poyntzpass before returning to Portadown; there were no longer any crossing facilities at Scarva. Looking towards Portadown, the substantial buildings on the down line have been demolished but the shelter on the up platform survives, out of use.

DJA Young

Goraghwood as seen from the cab of a railcar on a south-bound 'Enterprise' in 1963. The branch platform used by Newry and Warrenpoint trains is to the left of the station buildings. A 'Jeep' is hauling a north-bound train from Éire. The withdrawn vehicle in the sidings to the right is still in GNR(I) livery – it is one of their railbuses, converted from a road bus fitted with Howden-Meredith patent flanged wheels; it is now preserved in the Irish Railway Collection at the Ulster Folk and Transport Museum, Cultra.   *Craig Robb*

Coalisland, looking towards Cookstown. The attractive stone bridge had three arches which spanned the main running line, the loop and the sand siding. On the left of the picture we can just see part of the replacement signal cabin built in 1957. It consisted of a steel frame clad in red bricks.   *JD FitzGerald*

Pomeroy had the distinction of being the highest station in Ireland. The main station building, on the right looking towards Omagh, dated back to PDOJR days, and is typical of the style used by that company, but the signal cabin is a GNR(I) addition. Ex-NCC 'Mogul' No 91 is on a 13 July special to Donaghmore in 1964.

JD FitzGerald

Omagh station, taken from just below Omagh South cabin where the former line to Enniskillen left the 'Derry Road'. The INWR building sits proudly on the original platform; the GNR (I) additions to the station can be seen clearly. In the down platform, about to depart for Dungannon, is ex-GNR(I) 4-4-0 No 60 *Slieve Donard* on an Irish Railway Record Society tour on 13 June 1964.

TJ Edgington

The main station building at Newtownstewart, on the down platform, was a good example of William Henry Mills' architecture. Buildings like this, in yellow brick with courses of black, brown and purple brick, could be seen throughout the GNR(I) system.   *John Laird*

This view from a Derry-bound train, taken in June 1963, shows why Sion Mills often won the 'Best Kept Small Station' award. It was one of those stations where the name was spelt out in painted stones on the side of the bank.
                                                                                                        JD FitzGerald

In contrast to that at Newtownstewart, the GNR(I)'s station building at Strabane was in red brick with black and yellow lining, but still unmistakably in that company's style.   *John Laird*

Although Porthall station was one of those along the Derry Road which was actually in Éire, and consequently owned and manned by CIÉ, the station nameboard was in UTA colours of black letters on a yellow background. All passenger services here were operated by the UTA.   *JD FitzGerald*

Along the NCC

The NCC's Belfast York Road terminus had little architectural merit after the Blitz of 1941 and attracted little attention from photographers, hence this view taken in 1974. This was the only part of Sir Charles Lanyon's building to survive reasonably intact. *Brian Griffith*

York Road yard in 1962, seen from the footbridge which spans the railway. The original locomotive shed (below the coaling tower) had become a railcar shed in 1961. The track layout was further altered in 1965 when additional small steam locomotive sheds were built. Note the two very different types of water tower. Visible in the yard are blue ex-GNR(I) VS class 4-4-0 No 58, waiting to enter the works for overhaul, diesel shunter No 22, built by Harland and Wolff, ex-GNR(I) SG class No 44 in ex-works condition and at least two ex-NCC WT class 'Jeeps'. *JD FitzGerald*

This waiting shelter at Antrim is a good example of the style used by Berkeley Deane Wise in his designs for the NCC. It is still in use today and was extensively refurbished in 2001.

Ballymoney station was another of those designed by Wise. UG class 0-6-0 No 49 is sitting in Platform 1 at the head of a Portrush-bound enthusiast's special in September 1965. The first coach is in an experimental red livery.

JD FitzGerald

Looking towards Coleraine, this is Macfin, one-time junction of the closed Derry Central Railway with the main line. This typical NCC cabin dates from 1924 and replaced the two earlier ones. The chimney was rebuilt in the 1950s resulting in what must have been one of the tallest on a signal cabin in Ireland.   *RF Whitford*

This view of Coleraine shows the original BBCPJR building, designed by Sir Charles Lanyon for the railway's opening in 1855. It stood behind the up platform but was demolished in 1974.

After the BNCR acquired the LCR, it engaged John Lanyon to design new station buildings for that line. The main building at Limavady Junction was one such example. The station was further modified by the NCC, using some of its pre-cast concrete structures. Looking towards Coleraine, the branch to Limavady diverged to the right.

Drew Sucksmith

Ex-NCC 'Jeep' No 56 hauls a rake of ex-GNR(I) coaches through Trooperslane, which is being used as a temporary block post, on an up Orangemen's special. The building on the up platform (to the right, looking towards Carrickfergus) is one of Wise's most unusual designs whilst on the down platform is a typical BNCR shelter.

DJA Young

Downshire Park was one of those small NCC halts with short platforms and the most basic facilities. There are few traces of these halts nowadays. Downshire opened in the 1920s and was completely rebuilt in 1979. This view, taken from the up platform looking towards Carrickfergus, shows the down (Larne-bound) platform.

Drew Sucksmith

Ex-GNR(I) S class No 171 stops at Kilroot en route to Belfast with an early Railway Preservation Society of Ireland excursion. The station building, on the down platform, was built for the CLR in 1869 but has since been demolished.

DJA Young

Along the Bangor Line

The Belfast and County Down Railway's Queen's Quay station, looking resplendent after refurbishment in 1963. The workmen are clearing away the last of the rubble after the work which included removal of the balustrade around the roof and the canopy to the front.   *DJA Young*

Ballymacarrett Junction cabin was, in its last years, in the shadow of the Sydenham Bypass flyover. The nameboard is in the standard UTA colours of black letters on a yellow background, as used on many of their signs. Both the cabin and bridge have since been demolished.   *RF Whitford*

The BCDR provided this stationmaster's house at Holywood shortly after it opened the line in 1848. It was similar in style to some of its buildings on its main line, closed in 1950, but was destroyed by fire in 1965.

When the BHBR extended the railway from Holywood to Bangor they provided one through platform, later to become the up platform. On it they built this ornate wooden canopy with waiting rooms underneath; it survived until the late 1960s.

Ex-GNR(I) 0-6-0 No 47 passes through the down platform at Holywood with a special to Bangor on 22 July 1964. Trains such as these started on the former GNR(I) system and accessed the Bangor line via the Belfast Central Railway which closed the following year. This view gives us a good look at the down platform canopy, the signal box and the covered ramp which were added by Wise. Access to this platform was under the cabin.

Craig Robb

The Belfast, Holywood and Bangor Railway's station building on the up platform at Craigavad reflected the Italiante style of its Bangor terminus. The latter has gone, but Craigavad survives as a private residence and, apart from the removal of the small parcels office at the far end of the building, this view has not changed significantly in many years.

RF Whitford

A fine array of semaphore signals on the final approach to Bangor. This was the home gantry, replaced in 1980 by a colour light signal with theatre indicator, which protected the three platforms. The fourth post once carried the arm with controlled entry to the goods and carriage sidings. Apart from Portrush and Castlerock, semaphore signals in Northern Ireland are now a thing of the past.

NO Bailey

Below: The concourse of the seaside terminus at Bangor was typical of many important railway termini. The booking office is in the corner, with the main entrance to the left and the door leading to the refreshment rooms on the right. Also in view are the wooden kiosks which kept passengers well supplied with books, newspapers, tobacco and confectionery.

RF Whitford

DUNADRY

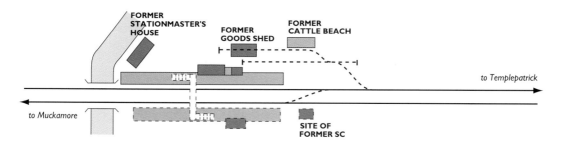

FORMER STATIONMASTER'S HOUSE

FORMER GOODS SHED

FORMER CATTLE BEACH

to Templepatrick

to Muckamore

SITE OF FORMER SC

Dunadry, opened in 1848, was another station built on an embankment. Its main building, also on the up platform, was similar to that at Doagh. The stationmaster was provided with a detached house, on ground level, near the station entrance. Dunadry closed in 1954, and the main building, footbridge and wooden down platform are no longer there, leaving only the privately owned stationmaster's house and the remains of the up platform.

Stations UK 27832

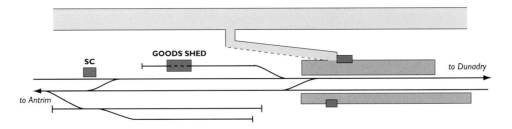

to Dunadry

to Antrim

SC

GOODS SHED

Muckamore was a much later addition to the timetable, in 1905. Just beyond were sidings which served the York Street Spinning Company works. The halt and cabin closed in 1963 and the concrete-faced platforms became hidden from view in the undergrowth. However, clearance work in connection with the reopening of the line has revealed them once again. The track, now single, has been realigned and now runs down the centre of the trackbed.

Stations UK 6118

ANTRIM

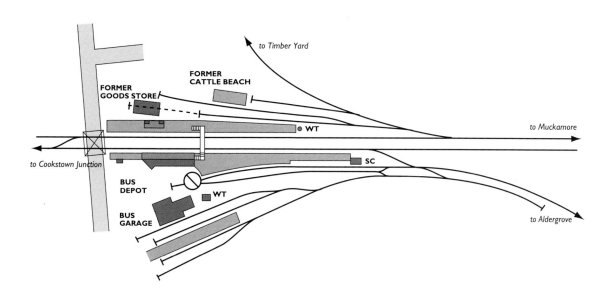

to Timber Yard

FORMER
CATTLE BEACH

FORMER
GOODS STORE

WT

to Muckamore

to Cookstown Junction

SC

BUS
DEPOT

WT

BUS
GARAGE

to Aldergrove

The station building at Antrim dates from 1901–2 and is a good example of Wise's architecture. This is a view of the main entrance, resembling a double-fronted mock-Tudor house, a view which remains much the same today. It opens onto the down platform; to the right of it we can see the UTA bus garage.

Behind the red brick and half-timbered facade was an extensive building in yellow and red brick. It housed the booking office and waiting rooms. Most of it was handed over to Ulsterbus in 1977 after NIR had moved their booking office to another part of the building, to the left of the main entrance shown in the previous photograph. A glass canopy covered the down platform. At one time it extended further along the platform, beyond the footbridge. It also provided shelter for the bay platform to the right which served GNR(I) trains from Lisburn. The footbridge came from Walter MacFarlane's Saracen Foundry in Glasgow. It once had a roof, the supports for which can be

seen at the top of the steps on the up platform. After being out of use for some time, it was finally replaced in 2001. Beyond the footbridge is the signal cabin, built in 1945 when the down platform was extended over the site of the earlier wooden structure. As the GNR(I) would not contribute to the cost of the new section of platform, the NCC only made it wide enough to serve their trains and put a fence along the back of it! The cabin was replaced in 1970 by a new one at the northern end of the platform, allowing the signalman to work the adjacent level-crossing gates. Behind the up platform, to the right of the photograph, a works train is sitting in the goods yard; a crane is included in the formation.

The shelter on the up platform, built in similar style to that on the down platform at Whiteabbey, still stands today. During refurbishment of the station in 2001, the waiting area was fully enclosed, the new frontage being in the same style. Behind is the stone goods store.

When Londonderry-line trains were re-routed to Belfast via Lisburn in 1978, this platform became unused. The track layout meant that trains could only access the branch from the down and bay platforms. Therefore, trains could not pass at Antrim, but as the line north of the station was double to Ballymena it served as a 'flying' loop. The station was resignalled in 1990 and the track layout altered to create a loop; at the same time the double track from here to Ballymena was singled.

COOKSTOWN JUNCTION

The branch from Drumsough Junction to Randalstown opened in 1848, at the same time as the BBR's main line. It was extended to Cookstown in 1856 and the name of the junction changed. Although passenger services over the Cookstown line ended in 1950 and the last branch line goods ran in 1959, Cookstown Junction remained open as a station.

It comprised an island platform, seen here looking towards Ballymena. The building located on it, looking rather dilapidated in this photograph, previously provided basic facilities. The posterboard on the left-hand side of the cable wall belongs to the Belfast Steamship Co and is advertising the services of its sister company in the Coast Lines group, Burns and Laird Line's ferry to Glasgow. The lamps mounted on pre-cast concrete posts have been fitted with electric bulbs; the station name was printed on the glass case. On the far side of the level crossing was an engine shed, by now disconnected and roofless, and a water tower.

In 1970 the platform was removed, allowing a much better track alignment for the main line, and new wooden up and down platforms built, one on each side of the crossing. The station's name reverted to Drumsough in April 1976, only to close six months later! All that can be seen today is a weathered nameboard on the down side.

KELLSWATER

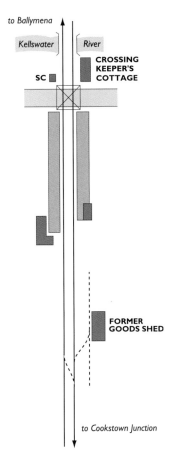

to Ballymena

Kellswater | River

CROSSING
KEEPER'S
COTTAGE

SC

FORMER
GOODS SHED

to Cookstown Junction

Kellswater station was open from 1876 until 1971 and, as can be seen, the facilities here were fairly basic. Looking back towards Cookstown Junction, the up platform is the wooden one; that on the down side has a concrete face. At the far end of the up platform, we can see the small pre-cast concrete goods store and the remains of the buffer stop on the former siding. Note the enamel 'Virol' advertisement sign on the platform fence, once a familiar sight at many stations. Only the down platform remains today, as does the nameboard on it. It is still in UTA yellow with black letters. The down line was lifted during singling.

Stations UK 6117

BALLYMENA

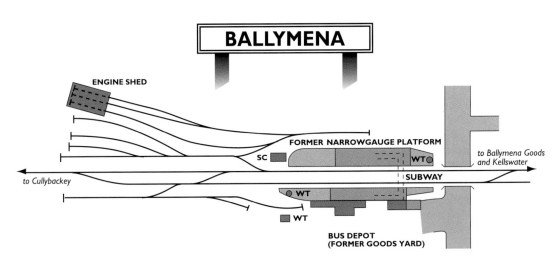

ENGINE SHED

FORMER NARROWGAUGE PLATFORM

SC

WT

to Ballymena Goods
and Kellswater

to Cullybackey

SUBWAY

WT

WT

BUS DEPOT
(FORMER GOODS YARD)

The BBR's 1848 station was at Harryville, half a mile south of the present one. Then, in 1885, the Ballymena, Ballymoney, Coleraine and Portrush Junction Railway opened its line between those points and provided a new station on the present site, although the goods station remained at Harryville. The BBCPJR was acquired by the BNCR in 1861 and its passenger station rebuilt by Wise in 1903–4, during the change from BNCR to MR(NCC).
It was Wise's last masterpiece; he retired due to ill health in 1906. The station also served the narrow gauge lines built by the Ballymena, Cushendall and Red Bay Railway and by the Ballymena and Larne Railway. Both had been absorbed by the BNCR in the 1880s. Prior to 1933,

boat trains ran to Larne Harbour over the BLR, enhancing the importance of Ballymena which was the largest intermediate station on the NCC. After 1933 they originated in Londonderry and ran on the broad gauge, using the 'back line' between Monkstown and Greenisland. The canopy to the front is a later addition. When the station was first built the entrance was to the side, where the nearest window is. There was also a large canopy along this side of the building to facilitate passengers alighting from carriages.

Immediately beyond the entrance was the booking hall, at ground level; the track was on an embankment. From here a ramp led to the down platform, whilst a subway and another ramp led to the island platform which served the up and the narrow gauge lines.
In front of the booking-office window is one of the railings which was once a common feature at railway stations. The clock is one of many which the Belfast firm of Sharman D Neill supplied to the province's railway companies. The poster below is promoting travel by Ulster Transport to the Royal Dublin Society's Spring Show and Industries Fair.

This view, looking northwards along the down platform, shows the extensive facilities provided, including a refreshment room with a marvellous bay window. It gives us a good view of the glass canopy which was similar to that at Antrim. However, at Ballymena canopies covered all three platforms and the building was entirely of red brick.

This is the ramp leading to the island platform. Belfast-bound trains departed from the left-hand face, narrow gauge trains formerly from the right. Both ramps and subway were lined with white tiles and were retained and incorporated into the present station, opened in 1981. Some of the wrought iron railings, seen protecting the ramps, have also been retained. But apart from these features, the new station pays at least a little homage to Wise; the main building reflects the half-timbered mock-Tudor style he used in so many of his designs.

The water tower at the southern end of the island platform, supplied by Cowan Sheddon Co of Carlisle, served both broad gauge and narrow gauge trains. It still stands today, the right-hand outlet being used by Railway Preservation Society of Ireland locomotives returning to Whitehead from Portrush and Londonderry. Once again the gas lights have been replaced by electric lights, but the original standards adapted. They also carry station nameplates.

The narrow gauge line to Larne ran parallel to the main line as far as Harryville (the goods station). However, the bridge at the southern end of Ballymena was rebuilt and narrowed, hence the disappearance of the BLR trackbed. At the far side of the bridge, the up starting semaphore signal is one of the somersault type favoured by the NCC.

A fine example of a BNCR/NCC signal cabin was built at the northern end of the island platform. This style was developed by Wise in the 1890s. It may seem, looking across the main line from the down platform, that this is the rear. Not so! The NCC often put the lever frame at the back of the cabin to give their signalmen a better view of the track – no lever frame between them and the window – hence the chimney in the front.

Right: Inside the cabin we get a good look at the lever frame and instruments. Looking along the shelf we see, on the left-hand side, a track circuit occupancy instrument to indicate if a train is sitting on a particular section of track. Next is one of the emergency switches, covered with a paper seal, which enabled levers with electric locks to be released in an emergency. If the seal was broken the incident had to be reported and a new seal fitted. To its right is the Tyer's block instrument which controlled movements over the double track to and from Kellswater.

In the centre is the track diagram (now in the author's collection) followed by another two track circuit indicators and three signal repeaters. At the far end of the frame is the Tyer's tablet instrument controlling the single line section to Cullybackey; the line north of Ballymena was always single. Above the tablet instrument a paraffin lamp is attached to the wall.

The position of the levers indicates that a Belfast-bound train is about to depart from the up platform. The cabin is extant but no longer used for signalling; Ballymena is now controlled from Coleraine.

CULLYBACKEY

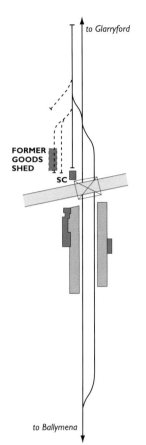

to Glarryford

FORMER
GOODS
SHED

SC

to Ballymena

When Cullybackey was opened in 1865 the BNCR provided this attractive red brick building, with black brick courses, on the down side. Looking towards Ballymoney we can see more concrete lamp-posts, now fitted with electric lights, each of which has a station nameplate. The main nameboard is also erected on concrete posts. There are a variety of UTA posters on the main building, and under the eaves is another enamel sign advertising 'Virol'. On the up platform, disused and overgrown nowadays, is a wooden shelter. Both platforms have 'somersault' down starting signals; to facilitate fast expresses to Portrush and Londonderry, the NCC signalled most stations on the main line for two-way running through the loops, creating fast and slow lines. The goods shed and a 'new' signal cabin (1929) were built on the far side of the level crossing.

The station closed in October 1976, despite some local trains to and from Belfast starting and terminating here, only to reopen in 1982. By that time the loop had been lifted, so all trains now use the former down platform only. The main building is still lived in today, in private ownership. A new shelter in similar style has recently been provided for passengers.

Stations UK 5815

Left: Here, at Cullybackey, is an example of the tablet exchanging apparatus installed by the NCC. These allowed mainline expresses to run through stations without slowing or stopping for a hand exchange with the signalman.

The goods shed in the background is extant, as is the yard crane beyond it but hidden from view here.

GLARRYFORD

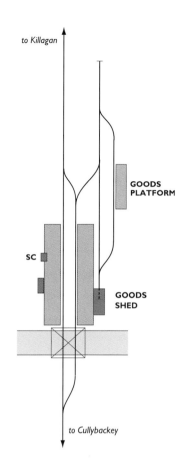

Glarryford was the next station and passing loop. This single-storey building, built from black whinstone and lined in red brick, was provided on the up platform, adjacent to the level crossing. The far end of the building, once again looking towards Ballymoney, contained the goods store. Note the station name on the lamps. There is also a fine array of UTA posters encouraging passengers to use its services to travel throughout Northern Ireland, or to book a through ticket to Great Britain.

On the down side of Glarryford we see our first example of a typical BNCR pre-1903 wooden shelter. This is a smaller and different style than those we have already seen at Whiteabbey and Antrim, but several of this type were built along the company's system. The signal cabin was situated further along this platform, to the right.

Glarryford last appeared in NIR's timetable commencing 3 July 1972, although no passenger services had been scheduled to stop there since 1971. The signal cabin and loop closed in 1967 but the platforms remain. The main building is still well maintained, now in the care of Glarryford Young Farmers.

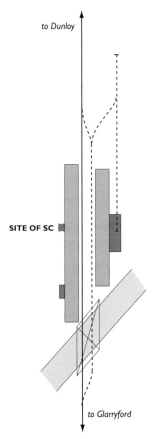

to Dunloy

SITE OF SC

to Glarryford

KILLAGAN

After traversing another level crossing, down trains entered Killagan, opened in 1855 as Bellaghy but renamed in 1876. It was very like Glarryford (which we are looking towards), having, on the up platform, a similar stone station building and, on the down side, another traditional BNCR shelter and signal cabin. The latter was destroyed in a bomb attack in 1957 and the loop and sidings were soon removed. In this view we can see the door in the end of the main building which allowed goods wagons to enter for loading and unloading. At the far end of this platform is a hut for the level-crossing keeper; all these crossings are now protected by automatic half-barriers.

On the down platform are some nice examples of NCC oil lights, again with the station name on the glass. There is also a BNCR sign, a few of which can still be seen along the line 100 years after the demise of that company.

Killagan closed in 1973 but the loop, on the up side, was reinstated in 1994. Both platforms are extant, as is the main building which is in private use as a store.

EM Patterson, CP Friel collection

DUNLOY

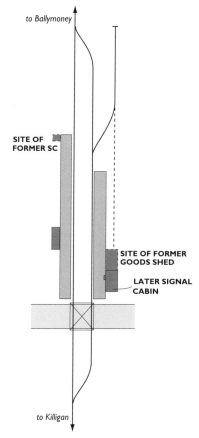

to Ballymoney

SITE OF
FORMER SC

SITE OF FORMER
GOODS SHED

LATER SIGNAL
CABIN

to Killigan

Dunloy also opened in this period – 1856 – and, as with the two previous stations, had a level crossing at the Belfast end. Beside the crossing, on the up platform, was the two-storeyed and cement rendered station-house. Attached to it was a stone goods store; all that remained of it when this photograph was taken was part of the wall. On the down platform was an unusually shaped shelter and, at the far end, a typical BNCR cabin. It was also destroyed by terrorists in 1957 and was replaced by a lever frame in the bay window in the main station building.

The multi-purpose diesel railcar in the down platform, but heading for Belfast, and with power car 65 at the front, is sporting the experimental maroon and cream colours introduced on the former NCC section by the UTA in 1965. They were later adopted by NIR for its first livery. Dunloy was another 1976 casualty. The loop has been lifted and the buildings demolished, leaving only the platforms.

EM Patterson, CP Friel collection

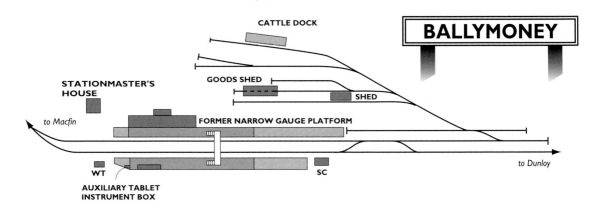

CATTLE DOCK

STATIONMASTER'S
HOUSE

GOODS SHED

SHED

to Macfin

FORMER NARROW GAUGE PLATFORM

to Dunloy

WT

SC

AUXILIARY TABLET
INSTRUMENT BOX

Although designed by Wise and built in 1901–2, therefore dating from the same period as Antrim and in similar style, the main entrance to Ballymoney does not look as attractive. Its appearance is not helped by the porch, a later addition.

The station underwent major refurbishment in 1990. The bay windows on the first floor have been replaced by ordinary ones, but the porch has been improved by the addition of a peak to the front. The right-hand wing has served as a pub for many years, more recently in the ownership of the late motorcycle ace Joey Dunlop, hence its name 'Joey's Bar'. The left-hand wing included the goods office.

Opposite bottom left: The concourse opens onto Platform 1, on the up side, which is actually the loop. Ballymoney was also the interchange with the narrow gauge line to Ballycastle. That line opened in 1880 and was taken over by the LMS in 1924. It closed in 1950 and an array of double- and single-deck buses occupy its former platform.

The signal cabin, seen in the distance at the Belfast end of Platform 2, was commissioned in 1929 and replaced two earlier cabins. When NIR introduced colour light signalling in 1989 the cabin closed. The new signals were initially controlled from a panel in the booking office but since 1994 have been worked from Coleraine.

Much of the wooden canopy was in a poor condition and removed when Ballymoney was refurbished, but at least the main building survived. At one time there were plans to replace it with a modern structure.

This view of the concourse has not changed much in the 40 or so years since this photograph was taken, apart from the glass partition which replaces the railing shown here. Beyond it, a UTA parcels delivery bicycle is sitting below a poster promoting travel to Great Britain via Larne–Stranraer on board the new TSS *Caledonian Princess*.

Amongst the services provided by the UTA, at booking offices such as this, were tickets on British European Airways and the opportunity to "insure your luggage here", as the sign to the right of the window advises us. The booking office now has a taller window but the small rail in front it is still there, now the only survivor at an NIR station.

Above right: A covered cast-iron footbridge led to Platform 2. The footbridge roof was later removed and the bridge itself is now closed off, a temporary structure being used in its place. Platform 2 is the fast through-line but is usually only used when trains are passing. The platform had an identical wooden canopy to that on Platform 1, backed by a full-height red brick wall. This canopy was also considerably reduced in length during refurbishment. These neat wooden waiting rooms and store were also demolished at that time. The attractive British Railways poster at this end of the building is advertising rail travel to Pembrokeshire. In order to reduce the time taken to cross trains, the NCC installed an auxiliary tablet-instrument at the Macfin end of this platform. This meant that the stationmaster could quickly issue a tablet to down trains for the Ballymoney–Macfin single-line section without waiting for the signalman to make the long walk from the cabin at the far end of the platform, thereby speeding up the departure.

MACFIN

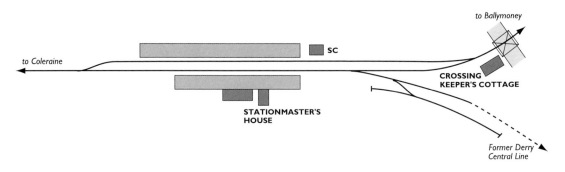

to Ballymoney

SC

CROSSING
KEEPER'S COTTAGE

to Coleraine

STATIONMASTER'S
HOUSE

Former Derry
Central Line

An early station was provided at Macfin prior to 1867, but when the Derry Central Railway opened in 1880 a new junction was created here. (The Derry Central linked Macfin with Magherafelt on the BNCR's Cookstown branch.) A new station, about half a mile down the line from the original, also opened in 1880. On the down platform was a red brick building, with yellow and black ornamental courses, designed by James Barton, civil engineer of the Derry Central. A stationmaster's house was provided to the left of this building. The Derry Central was worked by the BNCR from its opening and absorbed by it in 1901. DCR trains in both directions only used the down platform; there was no access from the branch to the up mainline loop. The DCR closed in 1950 but Macfin remained open, served by the main line, until 1954. The signal cabin and loop remained in use until November 1967 when the single line section became Ballymoney–Coleraine. This building still stands, albeit much altered, as a private residence, as does the detached former stationmaster's house. Both platforms also survive.

COLERAINE

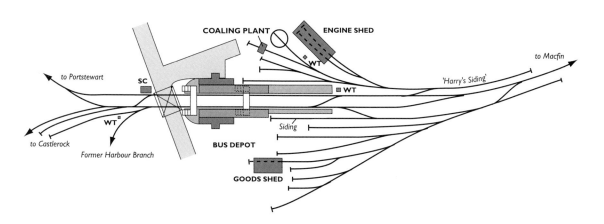

The railway from Londonderry reached Coleraine in 1853, two years before that from Belfast. However, the Londonderry and Coleraine Railway terminated at Waterside station on the west bank of the River Bann whereas the BBCPJR ran on the east side to Northbrook, the site of the present station. The original 1855 building was designed by Sir Charles Lanyon and was situated on the up platform. The Northbrook site was rather cramped, thanks to opposition from a neighbouring landowner, and had a level crossing at each end of the platforms. The two railway lines were linked in 1860 and Coleraine Northbrook became the joint station.

Derry Central trains also used Northbrook, which was becoming rather crowded. So, in 1882, the station was extensively rebuilt. The level crossing at the Belfast end was removed following expensive road diversions, the goods depot relocated and this new building was built on the down side. It was similar in style and appearance to Lanyon's original, but with some twin-arched windows, and is now listed. Most facilities were duplicated on both platforms but in UTA times Lanyon's original building fell into disuse. In latter years it was used for storage and departmental offices. It was demolished in 1974, the only surviving features being the bricked-up windows and doors in the wall backing onto the up platform.

The area to the right of this photograph is now occupied by the new integrated road and rail transport centre, opened in 2001, which is also built in this style and incorporates this building.

Left: The rebuilt Coleraine station had three platforms, two through ones linked by a footbridge, plus this bay (on the right) behind the up platform. The bay was used for the Derry Central trains which terminated here and has since been removed. In later years the canopy has been considerably reduced in length, not now extending much beyond the end of the building.

Opposite bottom left: Unlike those at other principal stations on the line, the footbridge at Coleraine was not covered. However, these rather odd-looking shelters were provided at each end where the bridge came through the canopy. They, and the bridge, have now gone and a new structure erected as part of the integrated transport centre.

This is another view of the platforms, this time looking from the up side towards the main (1882) building. Quite a number of passengers are waiting here and a number of luggage trolleys are lined up along the platform, no doubt awaiting the arrival of a train. Coleraine remains a very busy station and junction with trains arriving from Belfast or Londonderry (sometimes both together) and Portrush, passengers quickly changing and trains then heading off in two or three directions.

In the distance is the remaining level crossing and some of the colour light signals installed in 1938. For many years the crossing gates were operated hydraulically from the cabin, but they were replaced with lifting barriers when the station was resignalled by NIR in 1990. The level crossing is one of the busiest in Northern Ireland and actually has a road junction in the middle of it! The footbridge between the station and crossing allowed pedestrians to cross the tracks when the gates were closed against the road, but it was removed when the new barriers were installed.

Beyond the crossing a multi-engined diesel railcar is sitting on the track which led to the harbour; this was part of the original line through Coleraine and across the River Bann which provided the connection to the LCR. It was replaced by the present route through Coleraine in 1924. The harbour branch was disused from 1963.

Above: The number of signal boxes at Coleraine was reduced from four to two and then, when power signalling was introduced, down to one. The cabin stands on the northern side of the level crossing, beyond which we can see the chimneys on Lanyon's 1855 building.

The junction in front of the cabin is the point where the lines to Portrush and Londonderry go their separate ways, the rails on the far side leading to the seaside resort and those nearest the camera continuing on to the Maiden City.

This is the scene inside Coleraine cabin. The line was track circuited as far south as Macfin, a distance of five miles, but when Macfin cabin closed, and the loop was lifted, the track circuiting was extended right through to Ballymoney. This eliminated the need for a tablet on that section, movements being controlled by 'direction levers', but tablets were used from Coleraine to Castlerock and Portstewart. The illuminated panel indicated the position of trains. Points and signals were still operated by levers and the indicators on the shelf repeated the aspects of the signals and position of the points. Although the signalling was renewed by NIR in 1994, it is still controlled from this cabin – the levers being replaced by buttons on an illuminated panel – and it now controls the line up to and including Ballymena. Tablets are still used on the sections to Castlerock and Portrush.

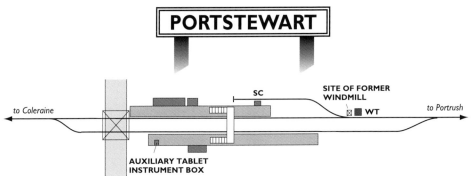

From Coleraine we will continue along the BBCPJR's main line to Portrush. Portstewart was the only intermediate stop. In fact, a local landowner, Mr Cromie, frustrated the railway's ambition of serving both Portrush and Portstewart, so this station was built 1¾ miles from the town. Cromie later realised his error and, from 1882 until 1926, the station and town were linked by a steam tram. It was replaced by a bus, the first example of bus substitution in Northern Ireland.

From 1960 the Coleraine–Portrush line was closed to regular services during the winter months. Portstewart station closed in 1963. Then, in 1968, the University opened on the outskirts of Coleraine and close to the Portrush branch. University Halt also opened and an all-year-round service resumed. In 1969 Portstewart reopened as Cromore, by which time the up loop had been removed.

This view is looking towards Portrush, with the level crossing, now an automatic half-barrier, behind the photographer. Beyond the fine basalt station building, restored recently as apartments after lying derelict for many years, is the footbridge, signal cabin and, in the distance, the water tank; the latter three have all since been demolished. Water was originally pumped into the tank using a windmill which stood alongside it but which was later replaced by a diesel pump. Although only 2½ miles from the seaside terminus, many locomotives were watered here as the quality of water was considered to be better than that at Portrush. Some camping coaches once sat in the siding behind the down platform but they were moved to Ballycastle during the Second World War.

In 1938 the up platform was extended towards Portrush, using pre-cast concrete sections. They were recovered in the mid-1960s and used to build the platform at University. There was also an auxiliary tablet-instrument at the Coleraine end of the up platform to speed the departure of Belfast-bound trains.

Various other interesting details around Portstewart station survived into the 1960s but have since disappeared, such as the little water tank which served the tram locomotives and this drinking-water fountain which was built into the stone wall of the station building.

Portstewart (Cromore) closed again in 1988. Another halt is served nowadays on the Portrush line. This is Dhu Varren which opened in 1969, on the outskirts of the seaside town, and is built on part of the Glenmanus siding where ballast wagons were once loaded.

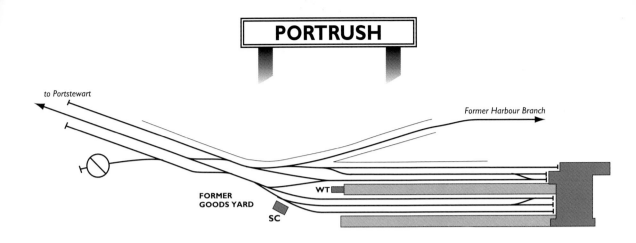

to Portstewart

Former Harbour Branch

WT

FORMER
GOODS YARD

SC

When the BBCPJR opened, Portrush was only a small hamlet. The arrival of the railway led to it becoming the leading tourist resort on the north coast. The small station was replaced in 1893 by one of Wise's finest designs. The contractors were McLaughlin and Harvey who still undertake work for NIR today. The impressive mock-Tudor building was in red brick and half timber and boasted a 50-foot-high tower with four clock faces, each five feet in diameter. Trams to the Giant's Causeway departed from just outside the building, on the road to the left.

To the right we can just see the wing which housed the refreshment rooms; they could seat some 250 patrons. This wing was demolished in 1970 but plans to remove the rest of the listed building were blocked. The surviving part of the building has now been relegated to the role of night club.

Inside, the concourse was well maintained despite the summer only service of the 1960s. It measured 100 feet by 60 feet and was covered by a roof supported on 'Belfast' trusses. Here we see the booking office, with another of those rails in front of the main window, and, beyond that, the entrance to the bar. The main station entrance was to the right of the booking office where the two bicycles are sitting.

Opposite was the platform barrier and this delightful kiosk. Although the main portion served as a shop, the left-hand wing was once the ticket office for the Giant's Causeway tram. The kiosk was later preserved by the Lord O'Neill and used for a while on his Shane's Castle Railway. It now resides in the Ulster Folk and Transport Museum's rail gallery.

The tower to the right of the kiosk contains another Sharman D Neill clock and a departure board on which details were written, in chalk, of "special return trains from Portrush today" – none on this occasion obviously!

Beyond the wooden barrier were three platforms; the gate to Platform 2 can be seen beyond the clock tower. The 'Belfast' roof extended along the first 200 feet of the platforms but was removed in 1960. The present station building, opened in 1974, stands on the far side of the barrier, behind the kiosk.

Our last picture of Portrush shows the cabin, still standing and now the last surviving mechanically operated NCC cabin. It looks rather weather beaten these days and is only used when traffic is unusually busy. The rest of the time the cabin is 'switched out' and the branch worked on the 'one engine in steam' principle. There are few special excursions to Portrush nowadays apart from the Railway Preservation Society of Ireland's steam-hauled 'Portrush Flyer'. Indeed, in contrast to the situation which led to the winter closure of the 1960s, traffic on the line is now busier in the winter months thanks largely to the University traffic. In 2000 the line was actually closed for the entire summer to allow it to be relaid without disrupting the University traffic, something unthinkable 40 years ago when the carriages from Sunday school and other 'specials' filled the platforms and yard.

Over the years the track layout at Portrush has been rationalised – the branch which led to the harbour closing back in 1949, although the bridge at the harbour remained in situ for many more years. The UTA removed the goods sidings, which once ran to the back of the signal cabin, to facilitate bus parking. After a further reduction in the size of the yard in the early 1980s, one of my jobs with NIR's Signals and Telegraphs Department was to draw a replacement cabin diagram – it highlighted the large number of redundant levers in the frame.

There have been proposals for some years to install colour light signalling controlled from Coleraine.

6 The NCC Main Line: Coleraine to Londonderry

Returning to Coleraine, we continue on our journey along the main line to Londonderry. As previously mentioned, the line from Derry opened in 1853 and originally terminated at Waterside station on the western bank of the Bann. A new line and bridge opened to connect it to the BBCPJR in 1860. It bypassed Waterside station which was subsequently closed. After giving cause for concern for many years, a new bridge on a new route, through the town and over the River Bann, opened in 1924.

The bridge has a lifting span to allow ships access to the harbour. This photograph is taken looking towards Coleraine station from the western side of the bridge. Immediately in front of the photographer is the lifting span and beyond it the operator's hut. The bridge is interlocked with the Coleraine–Castlerock section tablet instruments. Once a tablet has been withdrawn from the Castlerock instrument for an up train, the bridge cannot be opened until it has been

inserted in the Coleraine instrument. However, if a tablet is withdrawn from the Coleraine instrument for a down train, the bridge can be operated once the train has passed over a treadle mounted on the track between the river bridge and the 'Clothworkers' bridge beyond. Down trains are therefore not permitted to return to Coleraine.

Below the hut is the operating mechanism and a 250-ton counterweight to balance the bascule span. The original lifting mechanism was a Pelapole petrol engine with Hele-Shaw transmission, although in an emergency the bridge could be operated manually. It was replaced by the electric motor shown here in 1937, manufactured by Hugh J Scott and Co (Belfast) Ltd, and is still in use.

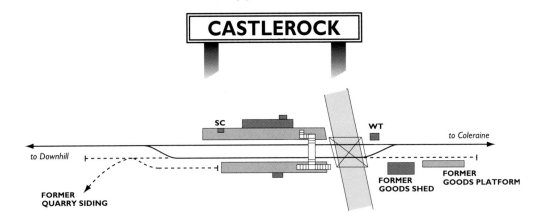

CASTLEROCK

SC
WT
to Coleraine
to Downhill
FORMER
QUARRY SIDING
FORMER
GOODS SHED
FORMER
GOODS PLATFORM

Below: The BNCR leased the Londonderry and Coleraine Railway from 1861 and fully absorbed it ten years later. Such was the poor state of the LCR's infrastructure that the BNCR had to renew much of it, including all the stations. In 1873–5 John Lanyon, son of Sir Charles, was given the task of designing the new station buildings. Most were built to the same basic style in red brick with ornamental lining.

Castlerock (1874) was the largest; it is now a public house. In the early 1960s the central portion of the building housed the station's refreshment room; a bookstall sat in front. The footbridge beyond was recently removed but, after a successful local campaign, restored and reinstated. In 1969 a new signal cabin was built by NIR between the station and footbridge. It is unusual in that it doubles as the booking office! Beyond the typical NCC level-crossing gates, mounted on concrete posts, we can see the water tower on the left and the goods store on the right. These latter three features have also gone; the crossing is now protected by full lifting barriers.

Opposite top left: Across, on the down platform, the BNCR provided another of its smaller wooden shelters, now sadly gone. The former siding at the Downhill end of this platform once housed some camping coaches; both coaches and siding had gone by the time these photographs were taken.

Opposite top right: This is the earlier cabin which was situated towards the Londonderry end of the up platform. Unlike the previous cabins we have looked at, the lever frame was installed at the front. After lying unused for six years, it was demolished in 1975.

Castlerock is now the last place on NIR, save Portrush, to use semaphore signals, although again there has been talk for some years about replacing them. Other proposals were to remove the loop altogether and install a new one midway between Coleraine and Derry.

DOWNHILL

to Magilligan   River   to Castlerock

Previous page, bottom: Shortly after leaving Castlerock, trains enter the first of the two Downhill tunnels, now known as the Castlerock tunnel, and 668 yards long. Soon after emerging from the second tunnel, 307 yards long, the former Downhill station is reached. This was a single-platformed station which, like most of the stations on this section, opened with the railway in 1853. The BNCR later added this neat red brick building. A camping coach once sat on an unconnected length of track beyond the platform, between the station and the river, at the Castlerock end. After being used in summer only for a few years, Downhill closed in October 1976. The station building had been demolished before then but the remains of the platform are still there.

As we can see in the distance, the Downhill Tunnel (as the second is now called) is constructed under the Mussenden Temple, a folly built by Frederick Hervey, Earl of Bristol and Bishop of Derry, in memory of his cousin Frideswide Mussenden (neé Bruce) who died in 1785.

Stations UK 27907

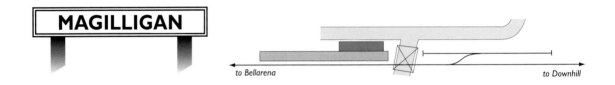

Between Downhill and the next stop, Magilligan, the A2 road which follows Northern Ireland's coastline crosses the railway at Umbra level crossing. Magilligan was another station with just the one platform, this time on the up side. The BNCR building, at the Coleraine end of the platform, has been extensively restored as a private dwelling and has featured in property magazines. The single-storey section at this end of the building has been converted to two-storey, the upper floor being built in the style of a signal cabin. Magilligan closed in 1976 but reopened briefly between 1980 and 1982. For a few months in 1855 a horse tramway operated from here to Magilligan Point.

Stations UK 27908

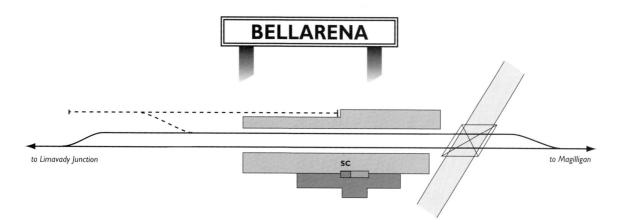

BELLARENA

to Limavady Junction

SC

to Magilligan

John Lanyon provided Bellarena with a slightly larger building than Magilligan, this time on the down side. Bellarena had the first passing loop after Castlerock but it was removed when the station closed in 1976. Unusually, the signal cabin was housed in the main building, where the bay window is under the canopy; the opening for the levers can be seen below the platform. To the left of the building, the A2 again crosses the railway on another level crossing. The station reopened in 1982 but only the down platform is used now; the up loop was not reinstated. The building is still lived in but an upper storey has been added to the single storey farthest from the camera, looking towards Londonderry. Unfortunately it is rendered in cement and spoils the appearance.

A pleasant feature at Bellarena, which is still there today, is this spelling of the station name in coloured tiles on the building's wall. Above it we can glimpse part of the oil lamp mounted on the wall.

LIMAVADY JUNCTION

The LCR opened between Londonderry and Limavady in 1852, but the extension to Coleraine nine months later left Limavady at the end of a 3½ mile spur. The junction was then known as Broharris Junction and no platforms were provided. Trains from Derry ran to Limavady and then retraced their steps to the Junction before proceeding to Coleraine.

The station building was built in 1875 on the island platform which served the branch and the main line. The up platform, on which the photographer is standing, was added later and was of prefabricated concrete sections and fencing. It was accessed by a covered footbridge and had a wooden shelter similar to that at Castlerock.

Passenger services to Limavady were replaced by a bus connection in 1950 and goods services ceased in 1956, but the junction station did not close until 1976. The loop was then lifted and the track realigned to give an easier curve.

Left: Here is a close-up of the wooden brackets which supported the roof of the main building and incorporated the company's initials. All that remains at Limavady Junction today are the platforms, footbridge supports and some sections of concrete fencing.

A number of airfields were built along the north coast of Northern Ireland during the Second World War. One such was RAF Ballykelly, just over a mile beyond Limavady Junction, where the main runway was extended over the railway by means of a level crossing. To prevent conflicting movements by aircraft and trains, a two-position block instrument was installed in the signal cabin, which was on the up side, linked to a second instrument in the control tower. The RAF left Ballykelly in 1971 – it is now the Army's Shackleton Barracks – and the level crossing closed. Another three-quarters of a mile brought trains to Ballykelly halt, opened in 1853 and closed in 1954. By the 1960s the single platform, on the down side, had been reduced to a mound.

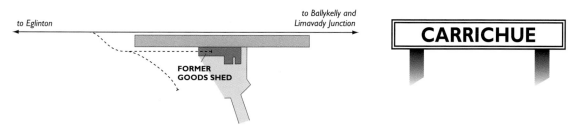

Carrichue, shown here looking back towards Limavady Junction, also opened in 1853 and closed in 1954. It too was in a very derelict condition ten years later, but the ruins of the building can still be seen behind the overgrown remains of the platform. The station also comprised a single platform on the down side with a small goods yard behind. The portion of the building nearest the camera was the goods shed; wagons could enter it via the door in the gable end.
Stations UK 27921

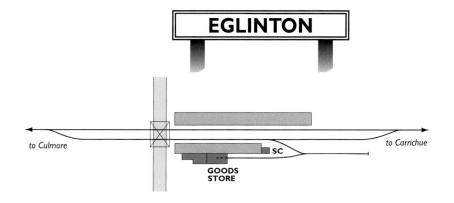

Eglinton was variously known as Willsborough and Muff in the early days of the LCR. It was given one of John Lanyon's buildings, on the down side, in 1874. Again, it was similar to the others on this stretch of line and had an integral goods store, rather like that at Carrichue. Looking towards Derry, beyond the somersault signals and level crossing, we can see that the up loop, with the gentle curve, was the fast line. On the up platform are some NCC pre-cast concrete lamp standards. Poor traffic prior to 1939 was made up for during the Second World War,

thanks to the station's close proximity to the Eglinton airfield. It was built for the RAF but mainly used by the Royal Navy and is now City of Derry Airport. In 2000 the main runway was extended right up to the railway track, so that once again there has to be coordination between trains and 'planes on this section of line. The station closed in 1973 and the building has been demolished, leaving just the platforms. The loop was also lifted and the track realigned.

Stations UK 27923

Above: Culmore had just a single platform, on the down side; the railway is right on the bank of the River Foyle at this point. The station opened in 1854 and lasted until 1973. Coolkeeragh Post Office was operated from the station building, which was at the Londonderry end. It has gone but the platform remains, directly in front of Coolkeeragh power station. The accommodation crossing at the end of the platform led to a jetty from where a boat once carried passengers to and from Culmore Point, on the opposite bank of the river.

Stations UK 27924

LONDONDERRY WATERSIDE

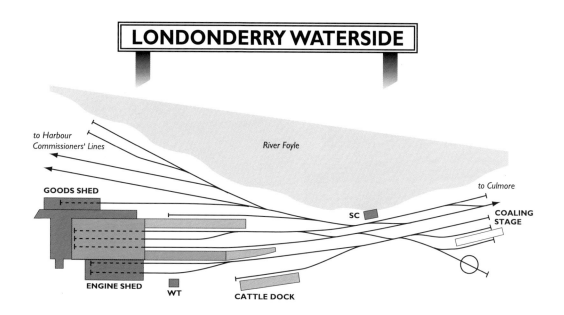

to Harbour Commissioners' Lines

River Foyle

to Culmore

GOODS SHED

SC

COALING STAGE

ENGINE SHED

WT

CATTLE DOCK

John Lanyon's Londonderry Waterside terminus was quite different to his other stations. It was built of dressed sandstone and opened in 1875. The Italianate-style tower was fitted with clock faces in 1884. The glass canopy once stretched across the full width of the building. Residential accommodation was provided, mainly at first-floor level. That for the stationmaster was in the left-hand wing of the building, not shown here, whilst separate accommodation

in the right-hand wing was used, in later years, by the District Engineer. The station was the target of a terrorist bomb in 1972 but was extensively refurbished by NIR, including construction of a new booking office and platform barrier. The work was completed in 1974, only to suffer greater bomb damage the following year. The central portion of the building was destroyed but, despite the construction of a new terminus slightly closer to the Craigavon Bridge in 1980, the remainder of the building has survived and has been renovated. The damaged portion has been replaced by a glass structure. The engine shed can be seen beyond the tower.

Above the archway in the tower the initials "B & N C Ry Coy" can still be seen. A 'BNCR' monogram was also cast into the gate which closed the archway.

Right bottom: Two platforms were provided at Waterside station and they were partially covered by an overall roof. The canopy which extended further along the arrivals platform, under which the photographer is standing, was added in the late 1930s.

Here, a multi-purpose diesel railcar, headed by power car 41, prepares to leave from the departure platform. From the late 1950s until the introduction of the 70 class diesel electric units in the late 1960s, these were the mainstay of services on the NCC main line. As mentioned, the MPDs also hauled goods trains; Waterside becoming busier following the closure of the GNR(I) 'Derry Road' in 1965 and transfer of cross-border goods trains onto the NCC. Between the departures platform and the River Foyle was the small goods yard and connection with the rest of Derry's railways, via the Harbour Commissioners' lines and the lower deck of the Craigavon Bridge. The NCC had another goods yard on the city side of the river, close to the GNR(I) station at Foyle Road. Nowadays trains run through the former Waterside goods yard to the new terminus. The canopy over the arrivals platform and much of the departures platform have gone, but the overall roof now covers Wright's Sofaland.

The concourse was most attractive, lined in various shades of brick. Much of the interior illustrated here was devastated by the bomb and, once the new terminus opened, there were suggestions that the whole building should be demolished, save the tower. Fortunately this did not happen, and today its role has changed from railway station to radio station; it now houses the local commercial station Q102.9.

7 The Larne Line

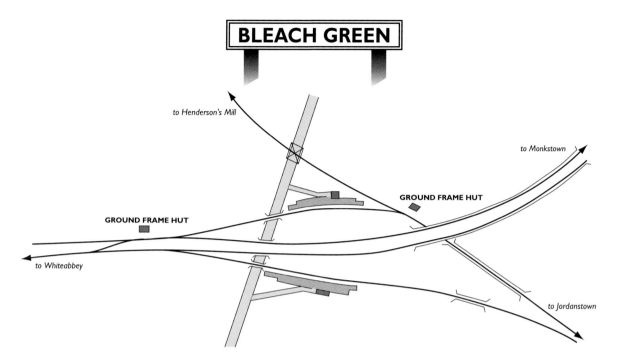

BLEACH GREEN

to Henderson's Mill

to Monkstown

GROUND FRAME HUT

GROUND FRAME HUT

to Whiteabbey

to Jordanstown

Larne-line trains also departed from Belfast York Road, running along the main line to Bleach Green Junction from where they went their separate ways. Immediately after the junction, but before the viaducts, was the halt.

Although it opened in 1925, along with many other halts on this line, it was rebuilt as part of the loop-line project using pre-cast concrete platforms and fencing. One unusual feature of the arrangements at Bleach Green was that you could not see one platform from the other; the embankment carrying the main line at the higher level between the up and down Larne lines blocked the view.

This photograph shows a multi-engined diesel railcar, headed by No 11, approaching the up platform from Jordanstown; it has just come off the original 1848 viaduct. The centre trailer is an ex-NCC non-corridor compartment carriage modified for use with the MEDs; it has manual doors whereas the power cars have automatic ones. The two tracks to the left are the main line; the down Larne line is to the far left, out of view, although we can just glimpse the down line viaduct amongst the bushes to the left of the rear power car.

DJA Young

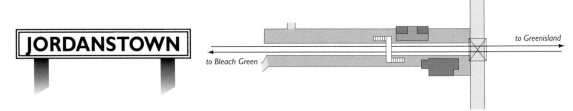

to Greenisland

to Bleach Green

This building, on the up platform, dates from the opening of Jordanstown in 1863 to serve a fast-growing exclusive suburb of Belfast. The BNCR offered 'villa tickets', giving free travel for ten years to anyone building a residence with a poor-law valuation of £25 or greater, within a mile of certain stations. We can clearly see that the platform has been raised at some stage.

Below left: On the down platform, in the 1890s, the BNCR built a large wooden shelter and waiting rooms. Beyond, at the Greenisland end of the station, the level crossing is protected by searchlight signals. To the left of the down starter is a telephone and a relay cabinet; relays are electromechanical switches which are operated by track circuits. They are responsible for changing the aspect of the signal and indicating the position of trains on the illuminated panel in the signal cabin. As we saw in our earlier look at Monkstown, the signal cables in the Greenisland area were suspended on wires at a fairly low level. At the level crossing we can see how they were carried across the road, suspended at a much higher level from telegraph posts. Jordanstown gained a new importance when the Northern Ireland Polytechnic (now the University of Ulster) opened nearby in 1974. Today, the footbridge and station buildings have gone, the latter replaced by simple shelters, while the level crossing now has an automatic half-barrier. All the NCC's searchlight signals have been replaced with modern two- and three-aspect signals.

GREENISLAND

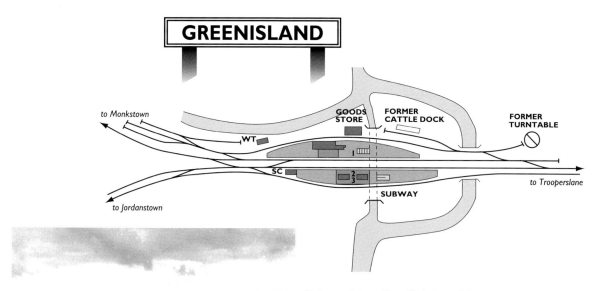

Below: Originally called Carrickfergus Junction, it was renamed in 1893 when the station was rebuilt. The BNCR provided the golf course on the Upper Road to help promote Greenisland. There were three platforms. The buildings on Platform 1 included the stationmaster's house. This platform was in effect an island as goods trains could run round the outside. To the left is the 1932 signal box, which controlled Greenisland mechanically, and Bleach Green Junction and the loop line electrically. Inside was a huge, illuminated, panel to show the signalman where all the trains in his care were. The cabin closed in 1986 when new signalling, controlled by York Road, was introduced between Bleach Green and Larne Harbour.

Above: This is the view of the junction at Greenisland as seen by the signalman from his cabin. The lines to the left are from Belfast whilst that to the right is the former main line, by then reduced to a single track and known as the 'back line', to and from Monkstown. The last scheduled passenger trains to use the back line were Londonderry to Larne Harbour boat trains in 1961.

Following the opening of the loop line, Platform 1 was used less frequently. Most Larne-line trains used the island platform which was accessed by a subway. In this view, looking towards Larne, the platform face nearest us was for down Larne trains whilst the far side was for up trains. This latter platform was curved and the track on a cant so that trains could run through at speed.

The semaphore signal beyond Platform 2 is one of the somersaults for which the NCC was famous. It is mounted on a concrete post; note the concrete block acting as a counterweight to the signal bracket.

The buildings at Greenisland were destroyed in fires in the late 1980s and replacements provided. It is still a manned station. During resignalling the Larne line was realigned to run through Platforms 1 and 2. Platform 3 and the express curve were removed.

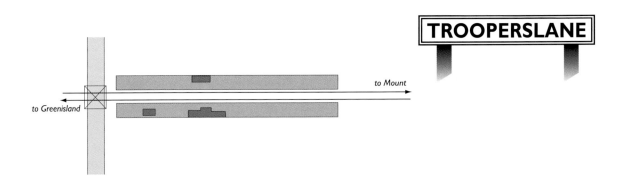

Trooperslane was another early station which, in 1896, was provided with a new building by Wise. He let his imagination run wild, the end result being this most unusual and attractive timber and brick building on the up platform. Sadly it has now gone, demolished in 1974. The station itself was due to close in 1977 but was given a last-minute reprieve. Small wooden shelters, similar to that which we saw at Glarryford, were also provided on both platforms.

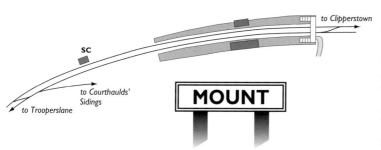

Below left: Mount opened as another of the 1925 suburban halts but only lasted until 1930. Then, in 1946, Courtaulds opened a factory nearby and the halt reopened. Courtaulds was also served by sidings, hence the modern signal cabin in the distance (looking back towards Greenisland). They owned two 0–4–0 saddle tanks built by Peckett and named *Wilfred* and *Patricia*. The main traffic to the factory was coal from Belfast docks and paper pulp from Larne Harbour. The sidings closed in 1967 and the halt itself in 1972.

The platforms were of pre-cast concrete slabs supported on brick pillars. The shelters were brick with concrete roofs and were similar to, albeit larger than, the many shelters later provided by NIR during their refurbishment of suburban stations in the late 1960s and early 1970s. The footbridge, from under which this photograph was taken, was a later addition, having been recovered by the UTA from the closed Tillysburn halt on the Bangor line. The station has been cleared away although a few remnants are lying alongside the track.

Stations UK 33331

Between Mount and Clipperstown, the Carrickfergus Harbour Junction Railway previously diverged to the south via a trailing junction on the up line. It opened in 1887, part of it using the trackbed to the original Carrickfergus station which closed in 1862. The Harbour Branch itself closed in 1957.

Just before the line passed under the bridge and entered Clipperstown halt there was, until 1957, a further siding, serving the salt works, this time on the down side. Clipperstown, like Mount, opened in 1925. It was just a quarter of a mile short of Carrickfergus' main station which can be seen clearly in the distance. Indeed, as shown here, the sidings of the main station once stretched right down to the halt. A brick-built shelter served the up side whilst on the down platform was a simple corrugated-iron shelter. New brick and concrete shelters were built in 1979, although they have since been renewed by metal ones.

Stations UK 5906

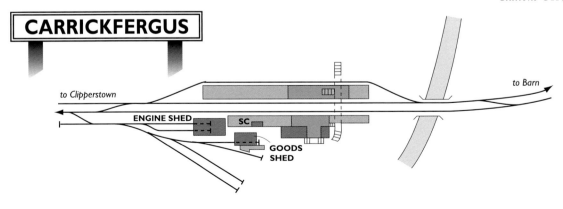

The BBR's 1848 terminus in Carrickfergus was on the outskirts of the town, situated on what later became the Harbour Branch. Then, in 1862, the Carrickfergus and Larne Railway opened and provided a new joint station on the present site. The CLR was later leased by the BNCR and acquired outright in 1890. The station was destroyed by fire in 1895 and replaced with this mock Tudor design by Wise on the up platform. It had three platforms linked by a subway. The loop through Platform 3 facilitated those local services which terminated at Carrickfergus, keeping them clear of the main running lines, although sometimes slow stopping-trains from Larne to Belfast were diverted into it to enable fast boat-trains to overtake them; a multi-engined diesel railcar can just be seen in this platform.

Looking along the up platform towards Belfast we see the signal cabin, the timber-boarded goods shed behind it and the engine shed beyond. Travelling along the Larne line today, Carrickfergus is the first example of a BNCR station on this route to remain largely intact. It was therefore appropriate that the NCC's war memorial was moved here, briefly, after the closure of York Road. The station building, which is now listed, underwent major restoration work in 2001. The open concourse area has been enclosed; a new glass partition in sympathy with Wise's architecture now fronts the up platform to create a more comfortable waiting area. However, one result of this work was that the memorial had to be moved yet again, back to York Road. Its new resting place is in the grounds of St Paul's Church of Ireland Parish Church.

to Downshire Park

to Carrickfergus

Half a mile beyond Carrickfergus was the first of a trio of 1925 halts, each just half a mile apart, serving more of the town's suburbs. These three halts were unusual in that the platforms were staggered. The platforms at Barn (briefy called, at first, Taylor's Crossing after the former level crossing) had concrete faces filled in with cinders behind. The footbridge is on the site of the former level crossing, removed when the road was diverted and raised on embankments and stilts before crossing the railway on an over bridge (behind the photographer); this view is taken looking towards Whitehead. Barn closed in 1931 but reopened during the war and these brick shelters with concrete roofs were provided. For many years the last train from York Road to Carrickfergus continued to Barn when required, returning 'wrong road' to the up platform at Carrickfergus before going back empty to Belfast. The halt closed again in 1977 and the platforms and shelters were removed in 1979, although the footbridge remains in use.

Stations UK 5812

DOWNSHIRE PARK

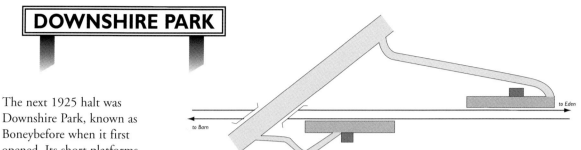

The next 1925 halt was Downshire Park, known as Boneybefore when it first opened. Its short platforms, which comprised a face of timber sleepers with compacted cinders behind, were staggered to an even greater extent – the corrugated-iron down-platform shelter can just be seen alongside the rear power car of the multi-engined diesel arriving from Whitehead. The railcar is in the maroon and cream livery introduced by the UTA and later adopted by NIR.

Downshire Park was rebuilt in 1979 with new platforms and shelters; the down platform now being closer to the up. 'Park' was also dropped from its name at this time. More recently, the bridge from which the photograph was taken has also been replaced.

Stations UK 33307

EDEN

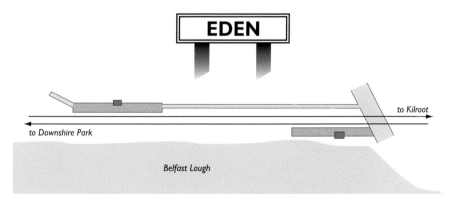

From Downshire Park, the railway runs along the coastline to Eden where the last of the 1925 trio was built. The same means of construction was used here as at Downshire Park, but the distance by which the platforms were staggered was even greater; there was quite a walk to the up platform which can just be seen in the distance. This view of the down platform clearly shows the use of pre-cast concrete for the single post carrying the station nameboard (the name was too short to justify the more usual two!) and the oil lamp beyond. Eden was closed in 1977 and the platforms have been removed.

Stations UK 5811

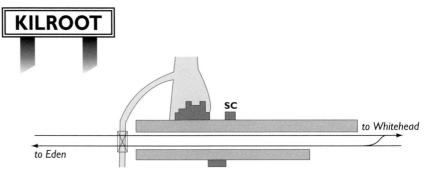

Kilroot opened in 1862 but had a shaky start with periods as a request stop and even complete closure. Then, in 1869, it was provided with this building on the down platform. It was designed by engineer Phineas Howell and paid for by Conway R Dobbs, a former chairman of the CLR and local landowner. The signal cabin was a later BNCR addition. Kilroot was the terminus for some local trains from York Road which were operated by the NCC's early petrol and diesel railcars, introduced in the 1930s.

Stations UK 33306

156

On the up platform, Wise erected a small waiting room in a style reminiscent of Trooperslane. The station closed in 1977 and the buildings were demolished two years later. The platforms have since been removed.

Stations UK 5810

WHITEHEAD

The first Whitehead station was built in 1863 on the Belfast side of the tunnel. It was replaced a year later by another close to the tunnel. The present station opened in 1877 but with one platform. It was designed by John Lanyon at around the same time as those on the former LCR, hence the similarity of the original portion of the building to Castlerock. The clock high on the post carries the name 'Ulster Transport' whilst the poster on the wall, outside the Gentlemen's waiting room, shows a drawing of a car ferry being unloaded at Stranraer. Whitehead was largely developed by the BNCR, thanks to the 'villa ticket' arrangements and its promotion as a destination for day trippers and holidaymakers. The railway invested heavily in projects such as the promenade and Gobbins cliff path.

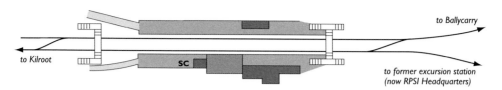

to Ballycarry

SC

to Kilroot

to former excursion station
(now RPSI Headquarters)

The growing number of visitors to Whitehead made expansion of the station inevitable. A second, down, platform was added whilst the building on the up side was greatly enlarged by Wise, as seen here. This canopy was built to create a large open, but sheltered, waiting area. More recently, part of it has since been enclosed to create a new waiting room. At the far end is the signal cabin, an unusually tall one to give the signalman a clear view over the station building.

This view, from the Belfast end of the up platform, shows the small wooden shelter on the down platform. The footbridge beyond replaced an earlier level crossing. An MED railcar from Larne, headed by No 15, is sitting in the up platform. Beyond the footbridge was Whitehead Excursion station, built in 1907. This was designed to take excursion trains off the main running-lines. It had an island platform, locomotive shed and water tower and is now the head-quarters of the RPSI. The NCC also provided a pavilion and tennis courts adjacent to the platform. Beyond Whitehead the track was single. The buildings at Whitehead have not changed much in the 40 years since this photograph was taken and in 1993, after years of neglect, were restored at a cost of £360k. There are now colour light signals, the footbridge has been replaced by a pedestrian level crossing, and the signal cabin, now disused, has lost its steps.

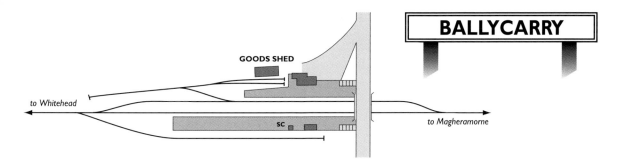

Ballycarry opened in 1862, at the same time as the railway, and was for many years the first passing-point between Whitehead and Larne. A substantial stationmaster's house was later added on the down side and a small station building on the up, just beyond the signal cabin. The goods store was used after the Blitz by the NCC's stores department. NIR later removed the down loop in 1970. The cabin and up platform building have been demolished but the stationmaster's house is now a private residence. All trains now call at the up platform which has been raised and given a basic open shelter.

EM Patterson, CP Friel collection

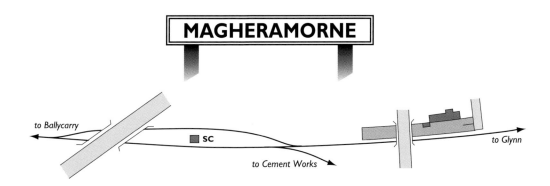

Magheramorne was opened in 1862 as Ballylig but was renamed the following year. The neat stone building and wooden shelter on its single platform were built later. They were demolished in 1979 and eventually replaced by an NIR metal shelter. Beyond the bridge, in this view looking towards Whitehead, was the last passing loop before reaching Larne. It was actually a quarter of a mile on the up side of the station. An interesting feature of the loop was that the typical NCC signal cabin, demolished after the introduction of power signalling in 1986, stood between the two lines. There were also sidings to the cement works, from which large quantities of bagged cement were loaded onto wagons for most stations on the NCC. The works also supplied the cement for the extension to Ballykelly runway.

However, Magheramorne's busiest and probably best remembered period was between 1966 and 1970, when the railway was awarded a contract to haul spoil from a quarry alongside the loop to the foreshore at Belfast to aid the construction of the M2 motorway. This contract helped prolong the use of steam locomotives in Northern Ireland.

Stations UK 5809

Right: The single-platformed station at Glynn, on the down side, opened in 1864. It was later given this impressive red brick and half-timbered mock-Tudor building by Wise in 1895, viewed here from the road.

to Maghermorne   to Larne

Here is the building as seen from the other side, looking across the railway track. It must have been one of the most attractive of the smaller BNCR station buildings but, sadly, it has been demolished in recent years.

Unfortunately the view from the station house was not the best; it overlooked the sewage works!

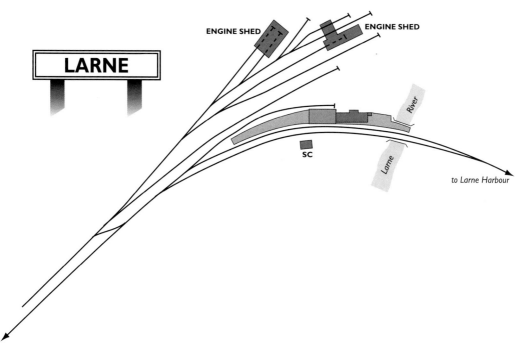

ENGINE SHED ENGINE SHED

LARNE

River

Larne

SC

to Larne Harbour

Right: Sir Charles Lanyon designed the Larne terminus of the CLR for its opening in 1862. It was, in fact, a through station with the platform on the down side. The tracks continued on to Larne Harbour to serve the 'short sea crossing', but this section saw little use until a regular steamer service to Stranraer was established. This is the exterior of Lanyon's original building.

Below: Here, looking back towards Whitehead, we can see the barrier rail and station building from the trackside. Larne had just one through platform, although a loop meant that goods trains to and from the harbour could pass passenger trains. Immediately in front of the camera is a fine cast-iron water column, fed from a water tank behind the station building. The wheel to turn the water supply on and off is situated beside the column, close to ground level. On either side of the column are signal wires and point rods from the cabin.

Inside was the booking hall and wrought-iron platform barrier. Above the window was a UTA notice giving details of fares on the Larne line.

Even after regular passenger services started running the extra mile through to Larne Harbour in 1872, many others continued to terminate at the town station. It was remodelled by Wise and this large island-platform building constructed. There was still just the one through platform, the track to the right, and a bay platform for trains terminating here, such as this multi-engined diesel railcar. It has an ex-NCC non-corridor coach as a centre trailer.

On the platform are various interesting artefacts. Whilst the station nameboards are mounted on concrete posts, the lamp standard is an earlier cast-iron column; interestingly the nameboard is one of the very few to have its own illumination. There are also some of the double-sided seats manufactured for use on island platforms; a couple of this pattern are now in the railway gallery at Cultra. In 1974 the line through Larne was pushed further out from the town, the new route allowing construction of a dual carriageway to the harbour, and the Lanyon/Wise station was replaced by the present Larne Town.

The railway between Larne Town and Larne Harbour had a very precarious beginning. It was built in the hope that Larne would become the Irish port for the short sea-crossing to Scotland, competing with Donaghadee on the BCDR. Despite the opening of the line in 1862, the cross-channel steamer was withdrawn at the end of 1863. The railway to the harbour was little used until the introduction of a new steamer in 1872. Some modest improvements were made to the original CLR station but in 1890 a replacement was authorised. By this time narrow gauge services were also operating to and from the harbour, via the Ballymena and Larne Railway.

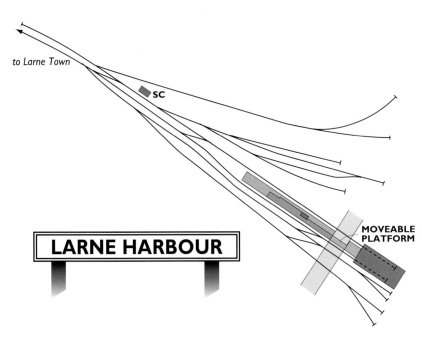

to Larne Town

SC

LARNE HARBOUR

MOVEABLE PLATFORM

Left: The new Larne Harbour station was Wise's first for the BNCR. It was very much a functional building comprising this large, uninspiring, wooden structure on the quayside. Once the BNCR was absorbed by the Midland Railway, and subsequently the LMS, it found itself part of one the largest public transport undertakings in the world. The parent company was also responsible for both the steamship services and railway connections in Scotland, a truly integrated transport system. Such was the efficiency of their operations at Larne that a ship could depart in under ten minutes after the arrival of the connecting train – something which has not been achieved for many years.

This efficiency was aided by the installation in 1931 of a conveyor belt which moved Post Office mails and passengers' luggage directly from the platform to the boat; the remains of it can be seen here, along the side of the building.

Inside the building, which was covered by a 'Belfast' roof, a ramp led from the quay to platform level. One unusual feature of the station was that it traversed a level crossing which separated the main building from the greater length of the platform. A moveable section of platform was slotted in across the level crossing, the position of which is marked here by the fencing which protected it, at the end of the main building.

Another unusual feature, long gone by the 1960s, was the clock which had two minute hands! One showed Irish time, once used by the railways here, and the other (25 minutes ahead) showed Greenwich Mean Time as used on the mainland.

The notice board indicates that the next arrival will be a train from Belfast and that there are two forthcoming Boat Train departures, the first to Londonderry via the 'back line' and the second to Belfast.

Stations UK 29830

Booking office facilities were provided in these wooden buildings, built in the style which Wise later made familiar throughout the BNCR. At the far end was a separate kiosk which sold newspapers and confectionery.

An island platform was provided. Looking towards the main building, the right-hand face served the broad gauge trains from Belfast and that on the left served the narrow gauge from Ballymena. When the narrow gauge passenger service to the harbour was withdrawn in 1932 that platform became a second for the broad gauge.
In 1967–8 the main building was demolished and replaced by a modern ferry terminal, leaving just the canopy shown here. Under this scheme only the left-hand platform extended across the road. However, this arrangement was short-lived and the level crossing was later abandoned, trains stopping short of the road. Another new passenger ferry terminal, fully integrated with the railway station, was built in 1985, this time on the inland side of the former level crossing. The remaining parts of Wise's station were removed and a new 'umbrella' canopy erected. In 1997 Stena Line, who now operate the ferry service from Northern Ireland to Stranraer, transferred their operation from Larne to Belfast. This resulted in the withdrawal of boat trains to Larne Harbour and, consequently, 120 years of rail and sea connections at the Co Antrim port came to an end.

Stations UK 29829

8 The Bangor Line

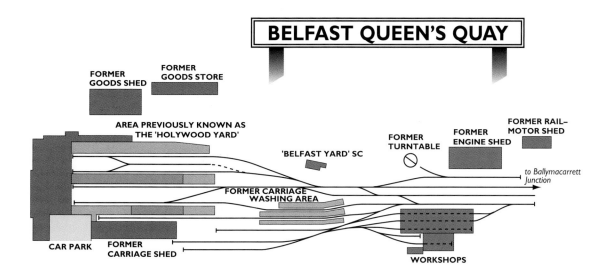

BELFAST QUEEN'S QUAY

FORMER GOODS SHED

FORMER GOODS STORE

AREA PREVIOUSLY KNOWN AS THE 'HOLYWOOD YARD'

'BELFAST YARD' SC

FORMER TURNTABLE

FORMER ENGINE SHED

FORMER RAIL-MOTOR SHED

to Ballymacarrett Junction

FORMER CARRIAGE WASHING AREA

CAR PARK

FORMER CARRIAGE SHED

WORKSHOPS

The Belfast and Co Down Railway opened its station at Queen's Quay, on the Co Down side of the River Lagan, in 1848 to serve its new line to Holywood. Two years later its main line was opened to Comber and Newtownards. This was later extended from Comber to Downpatrick and Newcastle with branches to Donaghadee, Ballynahinch, Ardglass and Castlewellan. The BCDR intended to extend its Holywood branch along the coast to Bangor, but this was frustrated by local landowners. It then planned a roundabout route, reaching Bangor via a branch from Conlig on the Donaghadee line. However, this idea was abandoned in 1861 when a new company, the Belfast, Holywood and Bangor, gained approval for an extension from Holywood to Bangor by adopting a slightly inland route.

The central portion of the BCDR's Belfast terminus dates from 1850 but when, in 1865, the BHBR acquired the Holywood branch and extended it to Bangor it built its own terminus at Queen's Quay, to the northern side of the existing station. The BHBR's line was leased to the BCDR from 1873, and was fully absorbed by the latter company in 1884. The two termini were then merged by knocking an archway from one to the other. Queen's Quay was extensively rebuilt in 1910–14. The BHBR terminus was removed (although the sidings and shed at this side of the terminus continued to be referred to as the 'Holywood yard' by the BCDR) and the two wings were added to the original building, in identical style.

The BCDR was acquired by the UTA in 1948. Two years later the UTA closed the entire system save the busy commuter line to Bangor and the Newcastle–Castlewellan branch, which lingered on until 1955, as the GNR(I) had running powers over it. At the time this photograph was being taken, in 1963, the UTA were giving Queen's Quay a facelift, hence the scaffolding. The canopy to the front and the balustrade around the roof had just been removed.

Above left: The ground floor of the right-hand wing was given over to the refreshment rooms. These decorative wooden and stained-glass partitions were situated just inside the main front-entrance, the nearest door leading to the bar and the one beyond leading to the café. The upper floor of the terminus housed the BCDR's headquarters, the windows above the bar giving a view of the concourse from the offices.

Above right: Here we get a rare glimpse inside the offices of a major railway station; this was the Secretary's office in BCDR days, later the UTA's audit department.

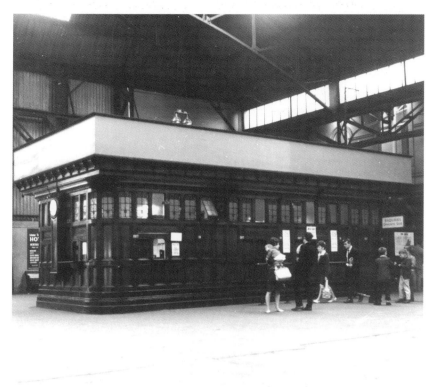

Left: The booking hall was situated in its own building on the concourse floor, near the Scrabo Street entrance. Some of the railings in front of the ticket windows can be seen, together with 'in' and 'out' signs. After the closures in 1950 it was really larger than was needed, so in 1967 it was replaced by a smaller facility on the ground floor of the main building, in the former stationmaster's office. The steel structure supporting the roof once extended for much of the length of the platforms. It was erected during the 1910–14 rebuilding and replaced the earlier wooden structure. The concourse looks rather bare in these photographs; in BCDR days there were vast floral displays throughout the station. Until their closure in 1954, electric trams entered the actual concourse of Queen's Quay. Like Belfast's other two termini, Queen's Quay was badly damaged by terrorist bombs in the early 1970s.

Opposite bottom: Looking from the main building across the concourse we see the wrought-iron barrier at Platforms 3 and 4. The wooden kiosks once housed, from left to right, a fruit shop, a confectioner, a tobacconist, and a bookstall. In this view the confectioners is being run by Empire in the left-hand kiosk whilst Leahy, Kelly & Leahy Ltd are selling newspapers and tobacco in the right-hand shop. Between the platform barrier gates and the kiosks we can see the manually-operated train-destination boards; the station names were painted onto metal strips which were slotted into the board. The clock is another from Sharman D Neill. Behind the barrier, multi-engined diesel railcars are sitting in Platforms 2 and 3. The advertisement for 'Harcourts Coal' has special significance to railway enthusiasts. The late Sir John Harcourt, a director of the firm and former Lord Mayor of Belfast, was the driving force behind the Transport Museum which opened in 1955. It was originally housed in the former railmotor shed at Queen's Quay. His sister, the late Mrs FE Breakie, Chairman and Managing Director of the firm, was also a member of Belfast Corporation and Chairman of the Museums and Libraries Committee at that time. The berths for Harcourts Coal were situated immediately in front of the station.

Above: The idea of a corporate carpet is not a new one! The BCDR had its own woven for its offices. At least one example survives in a private collection.

There were five platforms, No 1 being a shorter bay once used by the Holywood railmotor. Locomotive release roads were provided between Platforms 2 and 3 and between Platforms 4 and 5. Queen's Quay was the only terminus in Belfast to have them. In addition to the overall roof which covered much of the platforms, 'Umbrella'-type canopies provided further cover on all except Platform 5 (on which the photographer is standing).

In the early 1950s the UTA removed most of the overall roof, leaving only the portion over the concourse, and built a new section of 'umbrella' canopy in its place over Platforms 3 and 4. The track was also rationalised. The locomotive release roads, no longer required after the introduction of diesel railcars, were removed, as was the track to the 'Holywood' and goods yards and to the engine and railmotor sheds. Platform 1 could no longer be accessed from the main running-lines. The Platform 5 track and the remains of its loco release road were lifted shortly after this 1963 photograph was taken. That to Platform 4 was removed in 1974.

The Bangor line was the first in the UK to be fully diesel-operated. The specially designed trains are multi-engined diesel railcars (MEDs), introduced in 1951, which by 1953 were responsible for all services, apart from occasional steam excursions from the Great Northern via the Belfast Central line. The MEDs had automatic doors, some of the earliest trains in the UK to have these. Later, additional centre trailers, with the more traditional slam doors, were modified from older coaching stock. The MEDs gave sterling service until the late 1970s when they were replaced by diesel-electric railcars.

No 34 heads the railcar in Platform 5. The small flap at the front which is open on this car concealed the coupling equipment which allowed sets of MEDs to run in multiple. Note also the unusual window wipers on the driver's (centre) window. Two blades were fitted onto runners and they wiped the windows in a vertically downwards stroke. They were later replaced by conventional wipers. Power car 28 is at the front of the set in Platform 4, whilst No 24 heads the set in Platform 3. The even-numbered vehicles normally faced Bangor and had the guard's van at the end furthest from the driver's cab. Numbers 24, 26 and 28 were later fitted with a second driver's cab in a corner of the guard's van to enable them to run as single units, although this was not a common sight. Stored in the former Platform 1 we can glimpse one of the three ex-NCC non-corridor compartment coaches, modified for use with the MEDs. They only saw very occasional use as trailers on busy days such as 12 July and spent most of their time there. The passenger station was replaced by Belfast Central in April 1976 and advertised for sale as a warehouse, but there were no takers and it was demolished a few years later. The nearby workshops remained in use until 1994 as NIR's Central Services Depot. The entire site is now obliterated by the M3 motorway.

RF Whitford

BALLYMACARRETT JUNCTION

to Harbour Commissioners' Lines

to Ballymacarrett Halt

SC

Sydenham Bypass

to Belfast Queen's Quay

Belfast Central Railway

Former Main Line to Comber

In the early days, and up until the BCDR acquired the BHBR, the two companies had separate tracks running parallel to each other from Ballymacarrett to Queen's Quay. Later a junction was created, controlled by this cabin, not only between the Bangor and main lines but also with the Belfast Harbour Commissioners' lines and with the Belfast Central Railway. The latter allowed trains from the rest of the Irish railway system to gain access to BCDR metals.

The style of the cabin was not of the usual type for the BCDR. There were a couple of large ventilators on the roof but they disappeared in the 1950s. At the base of the cabin we can see that the wall above the opening for point rods and signal wires was supported by an old length of rail, complete with bolt holes! In its later years the cabin was overshadowed by the Sydenham bypass flyover which opened in 1959.

There were two major accidents near the Junction. The first was on the main line approach in 1871 when a Belfast-bound passenger train ran into a derailed locomotive. Although the locomotive was on an adjacent track it was fouling the main line and two passengers were killed. The more serious accident took place on the approach from Bangor on a foggy morning in January 1945. The Holywood railmotor ran into the back of a stationary commuter train from Bangor, stopped at a signal, killing 23 and injuring 41.

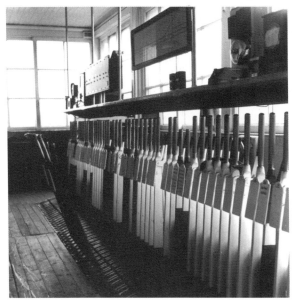

Ballymacarrett Junction cabin was, since the completion of automatic signalling in the 1930s, the last full-time cabin between Belfast and Bangor. The diagram in the centre showed the area controlled directly by the cabin, but beyond it is the illuminated panel which showed the position of trains between here and Craigavad, at which point Bangor took over. Alongside is the telephone linked to the automatic signals and installed after the second Ballymacarrett disaster. A display on the 'phone indicated which signal the driver was calling from.

A couple of the levers have had the tops cut off to indicate to the signalman that they operate electrical equipment, in this case colour light signals on the approach from the Belfast Central line, and that he does not need to apply the level of force he would use for mechanical signals or points.

At the back of the cabin was a large range and beside it, where the signalman is leaning, the desk on which all train movements were recorded in the ledger.

The Junction cabin was only about half a mile from Belfast Yard cabin (once the largest in Ireland) which controlled Queen's Quay. With the closure of the main line, the Harbour Commissioners' lines and, in 1965, the Belfast Central Railway, the two cabins were no longer required and both were replaced by a new one at Queen's Quay in 1966. The new cabin only lasted ten years, replaced by Belfast Central in 1976.

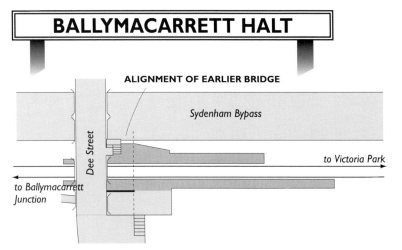

Opposite top: A quarter of a mile beyond the junction was Ballymacarrett Halt which had the distinction of never being provided with nameboards! It opened as a railmotor halt in 1905, and was once used by shipyard and aircraft factory workers in Queen's Island. This photograph pre-dates the era we are looking at, having been taken in 1956, but it is of particular interest as it shows the earlier Dee Street bridge. To facilitate the Sydenham bypass, which opened in 1959, it was replaced by the present bridge built to the far (Belfast) side of the original. Being a railmotor halt, the platforms were quite short and, like all those on the BCDR, were also quite low. The UTA raised them and built concrete extensions to both. In 1977 Ballymacarrett Halt was replaced by Bridge End, on the reopened Belfast Central Railway, but the platforms, the later bridge and some of the abutments of the earlier bridge remain.

Stations UK 5734

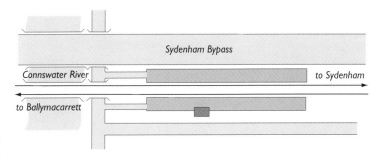

Victoria Park was another 1905 railmotor halt, and remained open until 1988. The platforms here were also extended but this time with wooden edging and compacted-ash behind. The original platforms are to the far, Belfast, end. A simple waiting shelter can just be seen on the up side. On the down platform is an automatic upper-quadrant distant signal, this one being on a typical BCDR lattice post but one which bore a plate claiming it for the London and North Western Railway! The lamp standards on the nearby Sydenham bypass are reclaimed trolley-poles.

In 1977, by which time the shelter had disappeared, the platform extensions were considered to be in a dangerous condition and removed. The original sections are still there.

EM Patterson, CP Friel collection

SYDENHAM

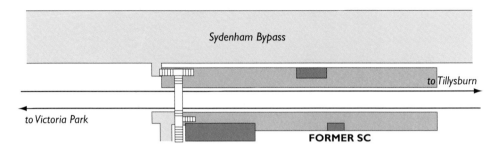

Sydenham Bypass

to Tillysburn

to Victoria Park

FORMER SC

Originally named Ballymisert and renamed Sydenham in 1856, this was the first intermediate station when the line opened. In 1870 the BHBR provided this stationmaster's house which was quite different to any other on the system. It survived for 100 years. The adjacent footbridge was once covered but has long since lost its roof. Old sleepers standing on end have been used to form a fence around the stationmaster's garden; fences of this type were used at various locations around the railway.

There are also a couple of old chimney pots on either side of the door being used as flower pots; they appear to be the original ones from the building as reference to earlier photographs shows that they were replaced at some time. During the Second World War a level crossing was in use beside the footbridge to give access to the Royal Naval Airyard; it was controlled by a ground frame.

Above left: The passenger facilities were added about 20 years after the house; the booking office was behind the window protected by the bars. Beyond is a very typical BCDR signal cabin. It was designed by GP Culverwell who succeeded Berkeley Deane Wise as civil engineer in 1888. Although closed since 1926 when the manual lower-quadrant semaphore signals were converted to automatic upper-quadrants, an economy measure, the cabin survived in good order for another 40 years.

Above right: On the down (Bangor-bound) side, the BCDR provided a waiting shelter to Culverwell's standard pattern, but much altered by the UTA who removed the small canopy to the front. Here the roof, visible from both the road and the railway, is being used to promote new and used cars by Marshall Watson of Sandy Row. Behind the platform is the Sydenham bypass and the Royal Naval Airyard, now Belfast City Airport. The station buildings were replaced by basic shelters in 1971, and in 1977 the footbridge was replaced by a new structure which also crosses the bypass. In 1983 the airport reopened to civil flights generating a little extra traffic for Sydenham.

TILLYSBURN

Previous page bottom: In the 1860s there was a short-lived station called Glenmachan, about half a mile beyond Sydenham. Another quarter of a mile brings us to Tillysburn Halt. Opened in 1880, this was the second to carry that name, the original being a short distance nearer Holywood. It was out of use for most of the 1930s and finally closed in

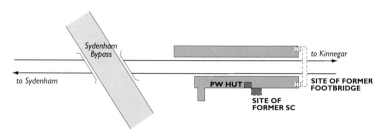

1945. The UTA later removed the footbridge for reuse at Mount on the Larne line. When this photograph was taken in 1964 both platforms were extant; today that on the down side is no more than a mound. Here a six-car multi-engined railcar, on a Bangor-bound train, has just passed under the concrete bridge which, from 1959 until 2001, carried the bypass over the railway. To the right of the railcar is a hanger at the airyard.

On the up platform are UTA and BCDR trespass signs and beyond is an upper-quadrant signal. The pointed end denoted that it was automatic. The cabin at Tillysburn, which was located on this platform, closed in 1925 when the signals were converted to upper quadrant and remotely controlled from Sydenham. Like those at Sydenham they became fully automatic in 1926. Along the backs of both platforms are upright rails which were used to support the picket fencing.

EM Patterson, CP Friel collection

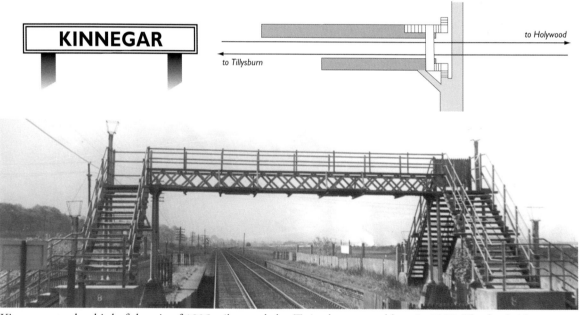

Kinnegar was the third of the trio of 1905 railmotor halts. Trains last stopped here in 1957. The footbridge survived for another 20 years and indeed the uprights still stand. The lamp standards are typical of many on the BCDR, comprising a length of rail fitted with a wooden cover onto which the lamp was fastened.

This view is taken from the cab of a Belfast-bound railcar as it crosses the accommodation crossing which is still in occasional use. Looking at this photograph, and travelling over this section of line today, it is hard to believe that the sea once came right up to the railway. Between Kinnegar and Holywood the area between the railway and the sea is now occupied by an Ordnance Depot. A siding connected it to the railway from 1940 until 1953.

EM Patterson, CP Friel collection

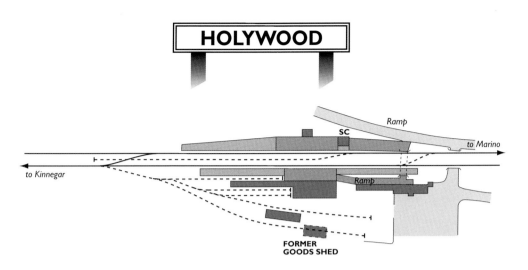

HOLYWOOD

Ramp

SC

to Marino

to Kinnegar

Ramp

FORMER
GOODS SHED

Holywood ended up with rather a hotch-potch of buildings, largely thanks to the belated extension to Bangor. They were all in different styles but well maintained and they combined to create one of the most interesting stations on the BCDR.

This was the stationmaster's house, built by the BCDR when Holywood was a terminus. At the far end we can just see the passengers' entrance, and beyond that was the booking office. This building was destroyed by fire in 1965 after which the UTA built a new booking office. It was only in use for a few years before NIR introduced conductors on their trains and Holywood became an unmanned station. The site of the stationmaster's house and garden later became a car park. And after lying derelict for many years, the booking office was demolished to allow a further extension to the car park; the palm tree in the former station garden was a landmark for many years.

A general view of Holywood from the up platform, looking towards Bangor. The building on this platform was provided by the BHBR whilst the down platform, canopy and signal cabin were added by the BCDR in 1886, to a design by Wise, when the line from Belfast was doubled. The signal cabin thus resembled some Wise later designed for the NCC, particularly that at Whitehead. For many years it had a curious lean backwards. Although automatic banner signals, such as that beside the cabin, were installed in 1931, Holywood cabin could still be switched in when required for local workings and goods traffic.

There was once a centre road. It allowed locomotives on local workings to run round their trains. To the right of the up platform is the bay once used by the railmotors. On the far side of the stone wall, which still stands, was the goods yard which has been obliterated by the Holywood through-pass.

A series of walkways, covered with various styles of roof, led from the booking hall to the platforms. Originally the platforms were at the same level as the building, but the extension to Bangor was at a higher level and on a new alignment. A single through platform (now the up platform) was built, but local trains from Belfast still terminated on the lower level. There is a record of passengers from Belfast to Bangor having to change trains at Holywood and go up some steps before boarding the Bangor train.

In this photograph was can see some newspaper billboards; the kiosk is just out of view to the right.

This is the view under the BHBR canopy with the Company's monogram visible in the roof. To the left were first and second class waiting rooms. The unusually shaped cut-out at the far end was to give drivers a better view of the signal ahead.

Here is a close-up of the gable end of the up platform canopy, giving us a good look at the BHBR monograms which survived until its demolition in 1973. One example is on display in the Ulster Folk and Transport Museum and another preserved in a private collection.

Right: The later canopy on the down side was a much simpler affair, with a semi-circular corrugated-iron roof and weatherboard wall. There was also a waiting room which survived until 1988 as an open shelter. At the far end was a semaphore signal which served as a wrong line starter, allowing local trains arriving from Belfast to depart from this platform on their return journey to the city.

From the booking hall, passengers walked through a subway, up a covered ramp and then under the signal cabin before arriving on the down platform; the lever mechanism was housed in cupboards to one side of the walkway.

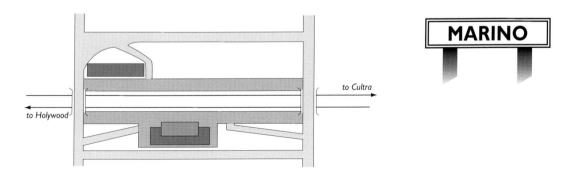

to Cultra

to Holywood

MARINO

In 1971 the track between Holywood and Marino was pushed out towards the sea to facilitate the construction of the A2 through-pass. It then passed under this Scrabo stone bridge and entered Marino. It opened around 1869 with one platform, on the down side, to serve the single track and the BHBR built a single-storey building.

When the track was doubled in 1900 a new booking office and waiting rooms were provided on the up side. The original building was given a second storey and became the stationmaster's house. A waiting room was provided alongside. Marino was closed by the UTA for a few years in the late 1950s and the up platform buildings demolished. The former stationmaster's house is now privately owned, access to the down platform being via the driveway.

Stations UK 5718

CULTRA

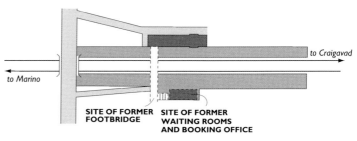

to Marino

to Craigavad

SITE OF FORMER
FOOTBRIDGE

SITE OF FORMER
WAITING ROOMS
AND BOOKING OFFICE

CULLODEN HOTEL GROUNDS
(FORMER BISHOP'S PALACE)

At Cultra, where the line passed through the Kennedy's estate, permission to build the railway was granted on condition that certain trees were left untouched, hence the sharp curves and steep gradients. The BHBR was obliged to provide buildings "of an ornamental character", so a small mock-Tudor-style building was erected. It was destroyed by fire in 1896. The BCDR replaced it the following year by this fine building in red brick with courses in black brick, viewed here from the driveway. The single-storey section housed the entrance and waiting rooms whilst the two-storey section beyond was the stationmaster's house.

Looking towards Belfast, the archway at the far end of the veranda led to an integral covered footbridge. It gave access to the up platform and also to the grounds of the Bishop's Palace, now the Culloden Hotel. It, and the waiting rooms on the up side, were removed after Cultra closed in 1957. The down platform building has not changed much in the 40 years since these photographs were taken, but although in private ownership it is now in a very poor state of repair.

Cultra reopened in 1978, primarily to serve the nearby Ulster Folk and Transport Museum which is situated in part of the former Kennedy estate. NIR made some efforts to retain the Victorian appearance of the station, even putting up a replica BCDR nameboard, but ten years later it was revamped in the 'Suburban' style with new shelters, signs and fences. Prior to reopening, the BCDR concrete coping stones, with their distinctive criss-cross pattern, were replaced with granite ones recovered from Goraghwood. A new footbridge was built at the Craigavad end of the platforms; it also gives access to the Museum.

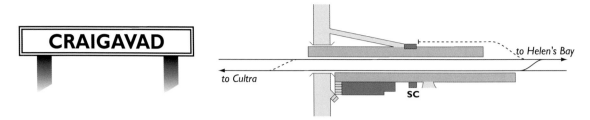

CRAIGAVAD

to Cultra ← | to Helen's Bay

SC

Opposite top: The building, in red brick with yellow brick lining, was on the up platform and reflected the Italianate style of the company's seaside terminus. The stationmaster's accommodation was on the ground floor, below platform level. The building was sold in 1976 and is another private dwelling. The arch to the left-hand end has been opened up as an entrance to good effect, otherwise this view is little changed. As previously mentioned, it bears some resemblance to Doagh on the NCC; Sir Charles Lanyon was engineer to both the BHBR and the BNCR.

Above: Craigavad was another station which dated back to the opening of the BHBR, and was the only passing place between Holywood and Bangor. At platform level the building appeared to be single storeyed. The archway led to the waiting rooms whilst the door further along the platform led to the booking office. It doubled as the local Post Office and was manned by the stationmaster. Sadly this aspect of the building is no longer visible as a solid red brick wall has been built in front. The smaller building nearest the camera served as the parcels office. The banner signal at the Belfast end of the platform is on one of the round posts which was specially erected for the new signals; most were bracketed onto the sides of the lattice or wooden posts used for the earlier semaphores.

Behind the photographer was the small but attractive cabin which was retained to operate the emergency crossover until it was moved further down the line in 1976. Across the line on the down platform was a small shelter and, behind it, the goods siding.

Craigavad finally closed in 1961 (it had previously been closed from 1957 to 1960), although trains continued to stop here occasionally for another 25 years to serve the nearby Guide camp at Lorne.

Seahill did not open until 1966, so our next stop is at Helen's Bay, the most distinctive station on the line. It opened in 1865 as Clandeboye, situated in the Marquis of Dufferin and Ava's estate and built at his expense. Benjamin Ferrey designed it in Scottish Baronial style and it contained a booking office, the Marquis's private waiting room and waiting facilities for ordinary passengers. Since 1978 it has been used, intermittently, as a restaurant.

Clandeboye was renamed Helen's Bay in 1885 when the surrounding area was being developed. A passing loop and up platform were added in 1894. The building to the right, which originally had a glass roof, covers the steps to the subway which leads to the up platform. It was given one of Culverwell's waiting rooms, replaced by a brick and concrete shelter in 1973.

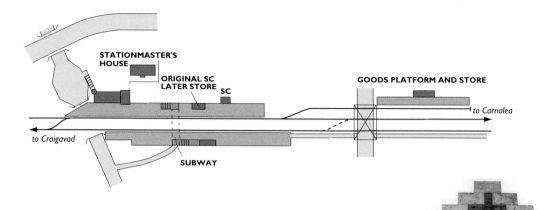

STATIONMASTER'S
HOUSE
ORIGINAL SC
LATER STORE
SC
GOODS PLATFORM AND STORE
to Carnalea
to Craigavad
SUBWAY

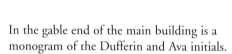

In the gable end of the main building is a monogram of the Dufferin and Ava initials.

A fight of steps led down to a courtyard, below track level. From here the coach path led in one direction to the nearby beach, and in the other to Clandeboye House, three miles away. The spire above the tower was removed by the UTA but was replaced in the 1990s. The staircase has been closed off.

At each end of the courtyard an ornate stone bridge bearing the Marquis's coat of arms was constructed. This is the bridge under the railway whilst that at the other end passes under Bridge Road and does not have the battlements. The coach path now forms part of the Ulster Way, a public footpath.

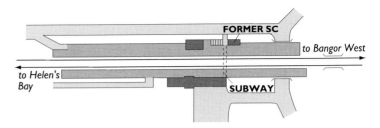

Shortly after leaving Helen's Bay the train passes over Crawfordsburn Viaduct, the largest engineering feature on the line. Beyond it was, between 1965 and 1997, Crawfordsburn halt (originally called Crawfordsburn Hospital). However, the next station we will look at is Carnalea.

It opened in 1877 with a single platform on the up side. A former brake van served as the station building. As on the BNCR, 'villa tickets' were available and they helped in the development of the area between here and Bangor. Carnalea was also a popular place for small, wooden holiday-bungalows.

Twenty years later, the BCDR constructed this new station building on the up platform, virtually identical to that at Cultra. This is the view from the road, the passenger entrance being the open door in the centre.

The main difference to Cultra is that the archway at the far (Bangor) end of the veranda led to a subway, not a footbridge. The single storey, which contained the waiting rooms and booking office, has been demolished but the stationmaster's house survives as a private dwelling.

On the down side, the BCDR provided another of Culverwell's waiting shelters and a low-set signal cabin, disused since the 1930s. Between the two are the subway steps. The cabin and shelter have now gone; indeed there have been three replacement shelters over the past 35 years!

The posters are advertising cheap day trips "to the seaside" (you can walk to the seaside within minutes from Carnalea station!) and excursions to Belfast and Scotland.

BANGOR WEST

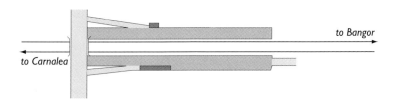

Opposite bottom: Bangor West Halt opened in 1928 to serve this rapidly growing suburb of Bangor; it is now the busiest intermediate station on the line. Looking towards Belfast, comprehensive facilities were provided in this small timber building on the up platform; there was a booking office, a general waiting room and, at the far end, a ladies waiting room. It was replaced in 1978 by an equally basic brick and concrete structure. There was a small shelter on the down platform.

The banner signal is mounted high on a lattice post which once had a semaphore signal on it. This signal was actually the Bangor advance starter and marked the start of the automatic signals on the up line. Looking through the bridge, it is possible to see that it has been widened and that the far section is a square structure in contrast to the arch on this side.

Previous page: For the opening of the railway, Sir Charles Lanyon provided the Belfast, Holywood and Bangor Railway with a single-platformed station at Bangor. The main building was designed in an Italianate style with red brick walls and yellow ornamental lining. The ground floor contained refreshment rooms and the stationmaster's accommodation whilst the upper floor, accessed through a pillared porch and flight of steps, contained the usual passenger facilities. Sadly, in 1950, the UTA modernised the original building by squaring the arched windows, plastering over the ornate brickwork and removing the porch, something regretted in later years.

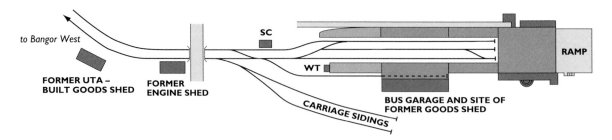

In 1890, shortly after it acquired the BHBR, the BCDR expanded the passenger station to three platforms. The area behind the main building was filled in to create a large concourse, covered by a 'Belfast' roof and surrounded by wooden weatherboard walls. A new entrance, to the side of the original building, was opened. The company's name was carried in bold letters on the veranda above this entrance.

After the Second World War, the deteriorating 'Belfast' roof was replaced by asbestos sheeting supported on a steel structure, and the veranda removed. The resultant appearance was of an unattractive 'barn,' as this seasonal view shows. Sitting alongside the main door is the taxi kiosk.

Some 20 years later, NIR rebuilt and improved this facade. The clock was not added to the tower until 1972; prior to this a Sharman D Neill clock, which also had a face inside the concourse, sufficed.

RF Whitford

Opposite bottom: The station boasted a number of wooden kiosks, such as this well stocked Eason bookstall. The billboard for *Radio Times* advertising 'Dr Who and the Web Planet' allows us to date these photographs with some accuracy. The first episode of this serial was broadcast on 13 February 1965. The kiosk is sitting on what was part of the single platform; the original station entrance was via the steps to the right of the kiosk, through the arch. Since the early 1950s they led to the bus station which occupied the former goods yard.

Immediately on entering the station by the main entrance (to the left of the photograph), passengers could buy their ticket at the booking office, built as a quarter circle. As the photograph shows, the entrance to the station bar was next to the booking office. When NIR opened a new booking office the original was refaced and was, for many more years, incorporated into the bar. The Post Office van is awaiting a delivery of mail from Belfast.

Centre: This is the view into the concourse, past the wooden ticket collectors' huts and through the wrought-iron platform barrier, which greeted passengers arriving on Platforms 1 and 2. In July 1964 Bertram Mills' circus visited Bangor. They came by rail, the train arriving in the centre (locomotive release) road. A welder was employed to cut part of the railing away to allow the animals to disembark from the end of the train.

The barrier and huts were removed in 1969 and a new building which incorporated the booking office, platform barrier and Eason's kiosk was constructed.

Above: Moving across to Platform 3, added by the BCDR in 1890 to the seaward side of the station, we see the original platform on the far side of the tracks. Behind it, under the canopy, is Platform 1 which was originally built as the goods bay. Between the main canopies and the concourse roof, we can see smaller canopies, supported on reinforced concrete pillars. They were erected after the Second World War to replace that section of the concourse roof which extended over the platforms. The replacement roof over the concourse can also be clearly seen.

It is worth noting the BCDR standard-pattern concrete coping stones on Platform 3, whilst on Platform 2 the original granite stones are used. Although all regular services had been operated by multi-engined diesel railcars for almost ten years, the locomotive release crossover has been retained in Platform 2 for steam excursions but removed from Platform 3. When the BCDR introduced the large 'Baltic' tank steam locomotives, a section of Platform 2 was cut back at this crossover to give them sufficient clearance. Although the platform surfaces have been raised this cut-out and the different coping stones can still, just, be seen.

The BCDR built a goods shed behind Platform 1. It was replaced in the early 1950s by a new shed further up the line, on the far side of the 'Boyne' bridge on the approach to Bangor and close to the engine shed. It was completed just in time for the withdrawal of goods services on the branch! As mentioned, the site of the original goods yard was then given over to the bus depot.

Opposite bottom: Our final photograph is of what became the last operational BCDR signal cabin. It remained in use until 1988 when new signalling controlled from Belfast Central was installed. It lay derelict for some years but was later demolished. The UTA had replaced the original lever frame with one from Magherafelt; after closure the Magherafelt frame was recovered by the Downpatrick Railway Museum and installed in their cabin (moved to Downpatrick from Kingsbog Junction on the NCC).

The small signals in front of the cabin, which look like miniature banner signals and which gave the same indications, are mechanically operated 'disc' signals used for shunting operations.

In the foreground is the track leading to the carriage sidings. They were used for holding stock on those days when steam excurions ran to Bangor on summer days, prior to the closure of the Belfast Central Railway in 1965. They were lifted in the late 1960s, no longer required after the loss of excursion traffic from the ex-GNR(I) lines.

Our look at Bangor concludes our tour of the UTA's passenger lines of the 1960s. It also highlights how much of our built railway heritage has disappeared over the past 40 years, Bangor being the latest casualty. In 1999 the station was demolished and over the following two years a new integrated road/rail transport centre was built on the site, although in this case the real damage had been done by the UTA 50 years earlier.

But perhaps it is equally surprising how much has survived. Indeed, at the time of writing in the aftermath of the Railways Task Force report, we are fortunate that railways have survived in Northern Ireland at all.

Bibliography

Coakham, Desmond, *The Belfast and Co Down Railway – An Irish Railway Pictorial*, Midland Publishing, 1998

Currie, JRL, 'Coleraine as a Railway Centre', *Journal of the Irish Railway Record Society, Volume 6*

— The Northern Counties Railway Volume I, David and Charles, 1973

— The Northern Counties Railway Volume 2, David and Charles, 1974

Fitzgerald, JD, *The Derry Road*, Colourpoint, 1995

— *The Warrenpoint Branch*, Colourpoint, 1996

Johnson, Stephen, *Johnson's Atlas and Gazetteer of the Railways of Ireland*, Midland Publishing, 1997

Johnston, Norman, *Locomotives of the GNRI*, Colourpoint, 1999

Kennedy, Mark, *The LMS in Ireland – A Irish Railway Pictorial*, Midland Publishing, 2000

Liddle, LH, 'The Derry Road', *Journal of the Irish Railway Record Society, Volume 6*

McAdams, NJ, 'Portadown as a Railway Centre', *Journal of the Irish Railway Record Society, Volume 6*

McCormick, WP, *Main Line Railways of Northern Ireland*, Author, 1948

McCutcheon, WA, *The Industrial Archaeology of Northern Ireland*, Her Majesty's Stationary Office, 1980

— 'Ulster Railway Engineering and Architecture', *Ulster Journal of Archaelogy Volume 27*, 1964

Murray, Kevin, *The Great Northern Railway (Ireland) Past, Present & Future*, Great Northern Railway (Ireland), 1944

Patterson, EM, *The Belfast and Co. Down Railway*, Oakwood Press, 1958

— *The Great Northern Railway of Ireland*, Oakwood Press, 1962

— *The Castlederg and Victoria Bridge Tramway*, Colourpoint, 1998

Journal of the Irish Railway Record Society, 'Irish Railway News', all articles 1955–2001

Irish Railfans News, all issues 1958–1974

Index to stations and junctions

Colour section references appear in *italics*.